Who Pays
the Property Tax?

Studies of Government Finance

Who Pays
the Property Tax?
A New View

HENRY J. AARON

Studies of Government Finance

THE BROOKINGS INSTITUTION

WASHINGTON, D.C.

Library of Congress Cataloging in Publication Data:

Aaron, Henry J
  Who pays the property tax?
  (Studies of government finance ; 2d ser.)
  Includes bibliographical reference and index.
  1. Property tax—United States. I. Title.
II. Series. Brookings Institution, Washington, D.C. National Committee
HJ4120.A62   336.2'2'0973   75-19270 on Government Finance. Studies
ISBN 0-8157-0022-9 of government finance.
ISBN 0-8157-0021-0 pbk.

9 8 7 6 5 4 3 2 1

For my mother

THE BROOKINGS INSTITUTION is an independent organization devoted to nonpartisan research, education, and publication in economics, government, foreign policy, and the social sciences generally. Its principal purposes are to aid in the development of sound public policies and to promote public understanding of issues of national importance.

The Institution was founded on December 8, 1927, to merge the activities of the Institute for Government Research, founded in 1916, the Institute of Economics, founded in 1922, and the Robert Brookings Graduate School of Economics and Government, founded in 1924.

The Board of Trustees is responsible for the general administration of the Institution, while the immediate direction of the policies, program, and staff is vested in the President, assisted by an advisory committee of the officers and staff. The by-laws of the Institution state: "It is the function of the Trustees to make possible the conduct of scientific research, and publication, under the most favorable conditions, and to safeguard the independence of the research staff in the pursuit of their studies and in the publication of the results of such studies. It is not a part of their function to determine, control, or influence the conduct of particular investigations or the conclusions reached."

The President bears final responsibility for the decision to publish a manuscript as a Brookings book. In reaching his judgment on the competence, accuracy, and objectivity of each study, the President is advised by the director of the appropriate research program and weighs the views of a panel of expert outside readers who report to him in confidence on the quality of the work. Publication of a work signifies that it is deemed a competent treatment worthy of public consideration but does not imply endorsement of conclusions or recommendations.

The Institution maintains its position of neutrality on issues of public policy in order to safeguard the intellectual freedom of the staff. Hence interpretations or conclusions in Brookings publications should be understood to be solely those of the authors and should not be attributed to the Institution, to its trustees, officers, or other staff members, or to the organizations that support its research.

Foreword

FOR THE PAST hundred years or more, critics have assailed the ad valorem taxation of property, the principal fiscal resource of American local governments since the seventeenth century, alleging that it is regressive and that it is administered inequitably. In 1931, the economist Jens P. Jensen wrote, "If any tax could have been eliminated by adverse criticism, the general property tax should have been eliminated long ago. One searches in vain for one of its friends to defend it intelligently."

Without assuming the role of friend or advocate of the property tax, Henry J. Aaron here examines the view that the tax is regressive and finds it in error. He acknowledges the validity of much of the widespread and persistent criticism of property tax administration, but argues that the administrative defects of the tax are remediable and not inherent.

In these senses Aaron's view is a new one. Pursuing it consistently, he recommends that tax administrators generally adopt the practice, now being followed in a few states and localities, of revaluing property more often and more accurately than in the past—even though owners who have paid, perhaps unknowingly, prices inflated by favorable property tax treatment are likely to oppose it. After concluding that the "circuit-breaker" laws of many states, under which homeowners (and, in some states, renters) receive partial or full rebates of property taxes paid, are unfair because they give the most relief to those in each income class with the greatest net worth, he recommends as a substitute a combination of income support payments and property tax postponement for households with low or diminished incomes.

Henry J. Aaron is a senior fellow in the Economic Studies program at the Brookings Institution and a professor of economics at the University of Maryland. He thanks Charles E. McLure, Jr., and Dick Netzer for detailed comments on the entire book, and Roy Bahl, Jesse Burkhead, Martin S. Feldstein, Edward M. Gramlich, Helen Ladd, Allen D. Manvel, Peter Mieszkowski, Oliver Oldman, Joseph A. Pechman, Robert D. Reischauer, Ferdinand P. Schoettle, and Mark Shankerman for helpful comments on various sections. He is also grateful to John Behrens and Thomas Vasquez for making unpublished Census Bureau tabulations available to him; to Philip Spevak, Mary Bell Hevener, and Melba Wood for research assistance; and to Marcia Mason for computer programming. Margie Barringer typed the manuscript; Evelyn P. Fisher checked it for statistical accuracy, and Mendelle T. Berenson edited it. The index was prepared by Florence Robinson.

This is the first volume in the second series of Brookings Studies of Government Finance. The first series, which was financed mainly by a grant from the Ford Foundation, was concluded with the publication in 1974 of the summary volume, *The Economics of Public Finance,* essays by Alan S. Blinder and Robert M. Solow, George F. Break, Peter O. Steiner, and Dick Netzer. Both series are devoted to examining issues in taxation and public expenditure policy.

The views expressed in this study are the author's and should not be ascribed to the trustees, officers, or other staff members of the Brookings Institution.

KERMIT GORDON
President

May 1975
Washington, D.C.

Contents

Appendixes

Index   107

Text Tables

Appendix Tables

CHAPTER ONE

Introduction

CRITICISM OF the property tax is a perennial feature of discussion about American fiscal policy. Books and articles on the subject regularly begin by taking note of this fact and of the remarkable unwillingness of the public to do away with so flawed a tax. Ten years ago Netzer wrote:

The American property tax abounds in anomalies. During the past century, no major fiscal institution, here or abroad, has been criticized at such length and with such vigor; yet no major fiscal institution has changed so little in modern times. . . . The demise of the property tax as a major factor in the American fiscal scene has long been heralded; yet it continues to finance more than one-fifth of the civilian general expenditures of federal, state, and local governments.[1]

These words apply today, modified only by the decision of numerous states to provide relief to taxpayers who allegedly bear unreasonable burdens from the property tax.

One reason for the continuing controversy is that in a nonagricultural economy the property tax is a poor index of both the public services received by households and businesses and the economic status, or ability to pay, of the taxpayer. In some communities,

1. Dick Netzer, *Economics of the Property Tax* (Brookings Institution, 1966), p. 1.

particularly small, homogeneous, residential suburbs, property taxes *are* good measures of benefits received from public expenditures and the rich *do* tend to pay larger property tax bills than do the poor. Yet most property taxes are used to pay for public schools and in general property taxes and numbers of school-age children are poorly correlated; and ownership of taxable real property and other indicators of income or wealth are not closely correlated. For these reasons, property taxes have not acquired the political legitimacy enjoyed by taxes that are perceived as better related either to ability to pay (such as income or sales taxes) or to benefits received from government actions (such as payroll[2] or gasoline taxes).

A second objection to the property tax is its alleged regressivity —the supposed tendency of the proportion of income paid out in property taxes to decline as income rises. The idea that families with low incomes must pay a larger portion of their incomes in property taxes than do families with high incomes had been generally accepted throughout the twentieth century.[3] Although some observers dissented,[4] the prevailing view in economic analyses and political statements alike had been that, through this tax at least, the poor do pay more. During the past decade, however, economic analysis has shown this notion to be incomplete, even with respect to that portion of the tax levied on housing; it now suggests that the property tax is probably progressive on the average, although some low-income families may be exposed to heavy burdens.

One of the objectives of this book is to explain this new view and thereby to improve public debate on the property tax. It also presents empirical results that show the property tax to be roughly proportional even under the old view. The primary purpose, however, is to shorten the lag between advances in economic analysis

2. The case of payroll taxes makes clear that legitimacy rests on perceptions, not on facts. Payroll taxes are perceived to be closely tied to social security benefits, but in fact the two are weakly related. See Joseph A. Pechman, Henry J. Aaron, and Michael K. Taussig, *Social Security: Perspectives for Reform* (Brookings Institution, 1968), pp. 107–09.

3. See, for example, Netzer, *Economics of the Property Tax*, especially chaps. 3 and 6, and app. E; Advisory Commission on Intergovernmental Relations, *Financing Schools and Property Tax Relief—A State Responsibility* (ACIR, 1973); *Building the American City*, Report of the National Commission on Urban Problems to the Congress and to the President of the United States, H. Doc. 91-34, 91 Cong. 1 sess. (1969), p. 358.

4. Harry Gunnison Brown, *The Economics of Taxation* (Holt, 1924).

and their entry into popular debate. Whether the property tax should be replaced or further modified, and whether tax relief should be extended, depends in large measure on how its burdens are shared. After chapter 2 has described the tax, the distribution of its burdens is examined in chapter 3.

The book also considers the charge that administration of the property tax is poor and should therefore be improved. Part of the controversy now surrounding the property tax arises because, alone among major taxes, it has a base that is not measured by tangible economic transactions, such as the sale of goods or services or the receipt of income. Because most real property is not sold each year but market values continually change, it is difficult to define fairness and equity in the administration of the property tax, let alone apply them. During the past decade, many proposals have been put forth to narrow the wide differences in effective tax rates paid by different property owners. These proposals call for larger increases in assessments on some properties than on others, a step that owners often vigorously resist. At the same time, prices of real property in many areas have risen rapidly, a development that requires commensurate increases in assessments if average effective tax rates are to be held constant.[5] In addition, during the 1950s and 1960s most localities were driven to increase effective rates as the desire for public expenditures grew faster than did property values. Furthermore, intervals between reassessments of property in most jurisdictions are rarely shorter than two or three years and sometimes run to decades. All these circumstances mean that property owners are periodically confronted with very large increases in property tax bills.

As an illustration, assume that a property was worth $20,000 at the last assessment, made five years ago. If overall prices have risen 5 percent per year, but the value of this property has risen 10 percent per year, the assessed value must be raised by 28 percent just to maintain the real value of taxes collected and by 61 percent to

---

5. "Effective" tax rates must be distinguished from "nominal" tax rates. Effective tax rates refer to the relation between annual property tax payments and true market value expressed as a percentage. Nominal tax rates refer to the relation between annual property tax payments and assessed values. A property with a market value of $40,000, assessed at $10,000 (one-fourth of market value) that is taxed $1,000 per year faces an effective rate of 2.5 percent and a nominal rate of 10 percent. Hereafter, unless otherwise specified, "tax rate" will always mean the effective rate.

keep tax as a percent of current market value—the effective tax rate—constant. Moreover, if, as is not uncommon, the assessor concludes that the previous assessment was, say, 20 percent below the appropriate rate and decides to correct his error,[6] the assessment on this property would have to double. A taxpayer who receives notice of such an increase may well be sufficiently perturbed to denounce the property tax, to cry for its reform, and even to allege its regressivity.

These and other forces have driven legislators to propose, and enact, programs of property tax relief. Numerous states and localities have expanded the variety of assistance to households deemed to suffer undue property tax burdens, and have made such assistance more generous. Former President Richard M. Nixon and Senators Edmund S. Muskie (Maine) and Charles H. Percy (Illinois) have all proposed that the federal government underwrite such relief.

In 1972 President Nixon requested that the Advisory Commission on Intergovernmental Relations study whether revenues from a federal value-added tax should be substituted for residential property taxes as the means of financing education. After careful study, the commission voted not to support the substitution. About the same time that these legislative and executive actions opened the issue of the role of the property tax in educational finance, the judiciary deepened uncertainty about the question. In the widely known Serrano case, the California Supreme Court held that the way in which the property tax was used to finance elementary and secondary education violated the equal protection clauses of both the U.S. Constitution and the California constitution; high courts of other states have found that other provisions of their constitutions have been violated. In an historic opinion, Associate Justice Lewis F. Powell wrote, for a six-man majority, that the use of the property tax in Texas did not violate the U.S. Constitution, but that decision has not stopped the steady flow of suits based on state constitutions.[7] The result of this vast and continuing litigation on school finance has been to heighten interest in alternatives to the property tax.

Both the poor administration of the property tax and its use to

6. This would be a modest error given current practice; see chap. 2.
7. *Rodriguez* v. *San Antonio Independent School District*, reported in *New York Times*, March 21, 1973. Also see Robert D. Reischauer and Robert W. Hartman, *Reforming School Finance* (Brookings Institution, 1973), pp. 58–59.

support elementary and secondary education raise the same question: Are there times when an unfair or inequitable tax should not be reformed because offsetting changes in market prices have already redressed the inequities to some extent? This question is addressed in chapter 4.

The most dramatic change in property taxation has been the widespread enactment by state legislatures of plans to relieve low-income households of some of the property tax burden they are deemed to bear. Building on the analysis of tax incidence developed in chapter 3, chapter 5 will examine these state plans.

A distressing amount of confusion has marked the debate over these proposals and over the place of the property tax in the federal system. Part of it flows from outmoded views of tax incidence; but part derives from the failure to distinguish two quite separate sets of issues. One set concerns the impact of budgetary decisions *by local governments* to change both property tax payments and local government expenditures. The other set concerns the impact of decisions to change the way given public expenditures are financed. For example, the federal or state governments may alter aid to localities; depending on whether such aid is curtailed or expanded, a given level of local expenditures will call for larger or smaller levies on local property.

In both cases the issues center on who will gain and who will lose from the proposed change—that is, on how residential or industrial location will be affected. But the problems that must be solved in answering them are quite different. This book will concentrate on the second question because the major current issues—federal or state aid for property tax relief, and changes in school-aid formulas occasioned by recent court cases—all involve the replacement of local property taxes by alternate federal or state taxes.

CHAPTER TWO

What Is the Property Tax?

THE PROPERTY tax varies widely across the United States. In 1972, 65,914 different governments had authority to impose them, and many of these jurisdictions overlapped one another in intricate patterns. Furthermore, all states allow subsidiary governments to set different rates and tolerate considerable local discretion in making rules and in administering nominally similar laws.

One can imagine a perfectly uniform national property tax, levied periodically on the value of all property in existence. It would fall on land, including natural resources, structures, machinery, consumer durables and nondurables, business inventories, government bonds, and cash. To avoid double counting, it would exclude stocks and corporate bonds, since these pieces of paper represent claims on tangible assets that are already taxed.[1] Such a base would come close to matching what economists have in mind by the term "capital." To levy such a tax at an equal ad valorem rate would require ascertaining the market value of all assets and setting the

---

1. In general, the tax base should equal the excess of assets over liabilities of the private sector. Thus, the base should include "outside" money—that portion of the money supply issued by the government in payment for goods and services or as transfer payments—but not "inside" money—that portion created through bank loans. See John G. Gurley and Edward S. Shaw, *Money in a Theory of Finance* (Brookings Institution, 1960), pp. 72–75.

nominal tax equal to the product of the effective tax rate and market value.[2] In practice the property tax is not so neat. First, all states exempt some real property from taxation because it is owned by governments, or by religious, nonprofit, philanthropic, or educational organizations.[3] However, the breadth of these exemptions varies, and an organization or person whose real property in one jurisdiction is exempt may be taxed on some or all of it in another. Second, the effort to tax business property other than land and structures differs widely. An increasing number of states exempt part or all of business inventories. In some states new plants are exempt, often for ten years or more, and in some so is property used to abate or control pollution. Third, the market value of property used by railroads and other utilities, banks, and mines is particularly hard to ascertain. Taxes on these properties are handled differently in the various states and are often calculated by methods different from those applied to other real properties. Fourth, the coverage of personal tangible and intangible property differs widely among the states. Only three states (Missouri, Arkansas, and Montana) claim to tax personal property (including motor vehicles) of households, businesses, and agriculture in full at normal rates. All others fully or partially exempt one or more of these classes of property.[4] Some jurisdictions claim authority to tax intangible property such as stocks, bonds, and cash. Finally, tax rates vary widely, from less than 1 percent of market value to 5 percent or more.[5] Beyond all this, the procedures used in assessing property and the efficiency

2. Whether property was "assessed" at its market value or at some fraction or multiple of market value has no bearing on the distribution of tax burdens. To collect an amount T, it makes no difference whether the tax is levied at the rate t on a property with a market value of V or at kt on the same property assessed at a value of V/k (where k is any number). In other words, the effective rate is all that matters; the nominal rate is completely unimportant.

3. The term "exemption" denotes all reductions in tax liability below that resulting from application of the nominal property tax rate to normal assessed values.

4. U.S. Bureau of the Census, *Census of Governments, 1972*, vol. 2, *Taxable Property Values and Assessment–Sales Price Ratios*, pt. 1: *Taxable and Other Property Values* (1973), table E, p. 9.

5. U.S. Bureau of the Census, *Census of Governments, 1972*, vol. 2, *Taxable Property Values and Assessment–Sales Price Ratios*, pt. 2: *Assessment Sales–Price Ratios and Tax Rates* (1973), table 12, pp. 110–43.

with which they are applied differ widely, so that the accuracy of appraisals is uneven. Thus, the ratio of tax to market value varies widely across and within jurisdictions.

As a result of such variations in law and administration, the property tax is far from uniform. In practice, it is very nearly a tax on real property only: 86 percent of the assessed value of locally assessed property is real estate.[6] Not all real property is covered, however; perhaps one-third is exempt.[7]

Trends in Property Tax Collections

Before World War II, the property tax had the largest yield of any tax in the United States. In 1934 its proceeds were more than double those of all other state and local taxes combined and exceeded total receipts of the federal government.[8] The subsequent growth of the federal and state governments, both of which relied on other taxes, reduced the importance of the property tax relative to other sources of revenue. As a fraction of gross national product, property tax collections fell from just under 5 percent during the 1920s to 2.6 percent in 1950.

Statistical indicators conflict on whether the property tax has become more important since 1950. Expenditures by local governments, the one level of government that uses property taxes extensively, have risen faster than GNP, and much faster than expenditures of the federal government. This advance reflected the surge in birth rates following World War II, because local governments pay a large part of the costs of elementary and secondary education. Despite a great expansion in federal aid to state and local governments, property taxes rose from 2.6 percent of GNP in 1950 to 3.9 percent in 1970, and from 11.9 to 13.6 percent of all taxes over the same period (see table 2-1). Because expenditures and taxes of state governments were rising even faster, between 1950 and 1973, property taxes fell from 46 to 37 percent of state and local taxes.

---

6. *Census of Governments, 1972*, vol. 2, pt. 1: *Taxable and Other Property Values*, table 2, p. 23.

7. See chap. 5.

8. Dick Netzer, *Economics of the Property Tax* (Brookings Institution, 1966), table 1-1, p. 2, and U.S. Bureau of the Census, *Historical Statistics of the United States, Colonial Times to 1957* (1960), series Y 254, p. 711.

Table 2-1. Relation of Property Tax Collections to Selected Revenue and Economic Items, Selected Years, 1950–73

Item	1950	1955	1960	1965	1970	1973
	Amount (millions of dollars)					
Total property taxes						
State and local	7,349	10,735	16,405	24,670	37,852	45,283
Local	7,042	10,323	15,798	23,836	36,726	43,970
All taxes						
Federal, state, and local[a]	61,783	87,504	126,252	184,241	277,376	347,742
State and local	15,914	23,483	36,117	56,647	94,975	121,102
Local	7,984	11,886	18,081	26,361	43,434	53,032
Revenue of all governments, total	66,680	106,404	153,102	225,547	342,489	426,172
Gross national product	284,769	397,960	503,734	684,884	977,080	1,294,919
	Ratio (percent)					
Total property taxes						
To all taxes						
Federal, state, and local	11.89	12.27	12.99	13.39	13.65	13.02
State and local	46.18	45.71	45.42	43.55	39.85	37.39
To revenues of all governments	11.02	10.09	10.72	10.94	11.05	10.63
To gross national product	2.58	2.70	3.26	3.60	3.87	3.50
Local property taxes to all local taxes	88.20	86.85	87.37	90.42	84.56	82.91

Sources: Gross national product—U.S. Office of Business Economics, *The National Income and Product Accounts of the United States, 1929–1965: Statistical Tables* (1966), table 1.1, and *Survey of Current Business*, vol. 49 (July 1969), table 1.1, and ibid., vol. 54 (July 1974), table 1.1.

Other data, except 1973—U.S. Bureau of the Census, *Census of Governments, 1962*, vol. 6, no. 4, *Historical Statistics on Governmental Finances and Employment* (1964), tables 2, 4, 6, and Bureau of the Census, *Census of Governments, 1972*, vol. 7, no. 4, *Historical Statistics on Governmental Finances and Employment* (1974), tables 1, 4, 6.

Other data, 1973—obtained directly from U.S. Department of Commerce, Social and Economic Statistics Administration.

a. Taxes; old age, survivors, disability, and health insurance revenue; unemployment compensation revenue; and charges and miscellaneous general revenue.

This decline was unevenly distributed among the states, however. During the 1960s, forty-seven states and the District of Columbia reduced relative reliance on the property tax (see table 2-2). In general, those states for which it had supplied the largest fraction of general revenues at the start of the 1960s reduced dependence on it most during the ensuing decade.

The relative importance of property taxation is associated positively with the percentage of expenditures for public education paid

Table 2-2. Change in Property Tax Collections as a Percentage of State and Local General Revenue, by State, 1962–70

Property taxes as percent of state and local general revenue, 1970	Increase, 1962–70		Decrease, 1962–70					
			0.0 to 4.9 percent		5.0 to 9.9 percent		10.0 percent or more	
	State	Per-centage points	State	Per-centage points	State	Per-centage points	State	Per-centage points
Less than 10	...	...	Alabama	3.7	Alaska	6.4	...	...
10.0–14.9	Hawaii	0.8	Arkansas	2.9	Kentucky	5.9	...	...
			Delaware	2.6	West Virginia	5.1		
			Louisiana	2.6				
			Mississippi	4.8				
			New Mexico	2.4				
			South Carolina	1.7				
15.0–19.9	...	...	Georgia	1.7	District of Columbia	5.5	...	...
			North Carolina	2.5	Tennessee	5.4		
			Oklahoma	2.8	Virginia	5.0		
20.0–24.9	Nevada	0.6	...	...	Florida	6.3	...	...
	Washington	1.6			Idaho	8.1		
					Maryland	7.3		
					Pennsylvania	5.1		
					Utah	8.5		
					Vermont	5.6		
					Wyoming	4.0		

25.0–29.9	...	Missouri	3.5	Arizona	6.9	Minnesota	13.9
		Oregon	1.7	Colorado	5.3		
				Michigan	8.6		
				New York	8.4		
				North Dakota	5.6		
				Rhode Island	9.6		
				Texas	5.5		
30.0–34.9	...	Montana	4.6	California	5.5	Illinois	10.7
		South Dakota	2.1	Indiana	8.6	Nebraska	12.6
				Iowa	7.7	Wisconsin	10.0
				Kansas	6.9		
				Maine	7.1		
				Ohio	5.2		
35.0–39.9	...	Connecticut	4.5	...		Massachusetts	10.8
40.0–49.9	...	New Hampshire	2.6	...		New Jersey	10.2

Source: Advisory Commission on Intergovernmental Relations, *State-Local Finances: Significant Features and Suggested Legislation, 1972 Edition* (ACIR, 1972), table 12, p. 28.

for by local governments (see table 2-3). This percentage varies from 0 in Hawaii to 97 in New Hampshire. For similar reasons, states in which local governments are responsible for a relatively wide range of services impose relatively heavy property taxes. States with relatively high property taxes tend to collect less than the average through other taxes but to have tax burdens larger than the average. The correlation between the proportion of personal income claimed by property taxes in 1971 and other taxes as a percentage of income was negative, and statistically significant.[9]

The foregoing statistics make several points. First, property tax collections are an important indicator of the relative importance of local government and, more specifically, of local responsibility for education. While logic does not require that local governments depend on property taxes or that all property taxes flow to local governments, any major shift in responsibilities for public education to higher governmental levels would probably signal the relative decline of property taxes.[10] Second, less property taxation means more of other taxes or fewer public expenditures or both. Third, property taxes have become less important in state and local finance at the same time that they have maintained their position in the national revenue system and grown relative to national product. The stabilization of the school-age population and the possibility of absolute declines make it extremely likely that the relative importance of the property tax will drop from the peaks reached around 1970 until at least the early 1980s.

Administration

The impact of the property tax depends on the vagaries of administration more than does that of any other tax. The base of nearly all state income taxes closely resembles that of the federal personal

---

9. Regressing property tax as a percentage of state personal income, P, on other state and local taxes as a percentage of state personal income, T, yields
$$P = 8.8 - 0.59T.$$
$$\bar{R}^2 = 0.29.$$
10. The decline need not occur if property taxes are converted from a local into a state levy. In 1973, 3 percent of property taxes, in fact, accrued to state governments. On this subject, see Robert D. Reischauer and Robert W. Hartman, *Reforming School Finance* (Brookings Institution, 1973), pp. 51–53, 92.

Table 2-3. **Relation between Property Taxes and Source of Local School Finance, 1969–70**

Local funds expended for local schools as percent of combined state-local funds expended, 1969–70	Property taxes as percent of state and local general revenue, 1970						
	0–10	10.0–14.9	15.0–19.9	20.0–24.9	25.0–29.9	30.0–34.9	35.0 and above
0–19.9	Alaska	Hawaii	...	...	...	...	...
20–39.9	Alabama	Kentucky Louisiana Mississippi New Mexico South Carolina West Virginia	North Carolina	Florida	...	...	...
40.0–59.9	...	Arkansas Delaware	Georgia Oklahoma Tennessee Virginia	Idaho Nevada Pennsylvania Utah Vermont Washington	Arizona New York Texas	Maine	...
60.0–79.9	...	...	...	Maryland Wyoming	Colorado Michigan Minnesota Missouri North Dakota Oregon	California Illinois Indiana Iowa Kansas Montana Ohio Rhode Island Wisconsin	Connecticut Massachusetts New Jersey
80.0–100	...	...	...	...	...	Nebraska South Dakota	New Hampshire

Source: Advisory Commission on Intergovernmental Relations, *State-Local Finances: Significant Features and Suggested Legislation, 1972 Edition*, table 12, p. 28, and table 54, p. 131.

income tax although effective rates vary widely.[11] Sales tax bases also differ considerably from one another because of variations in the treatment of food, medicines, services, and business purchases, and their rates varied from 3 percent to 7 percent in 1973.[12] However, an increase in taxable income or sales is fairly certain to cause an increase in tax liability. By contrast, the property tax is levied on estimated values, not on values reported in actual sales; consequently, changes in property values lead to changes in property tax liabilities only after an assessor changes his estimate of taxable value, a process that may occur virtually instantly or only after decades. Furthermore, effective rates and coverage differ widely not only among, but within, states.

The conventional measures of administrative efficiency are based on the ratio of assessed values, used for apportioning property taxes, to market values, expressed in prices of arm's-length sales. If the ratio of assessed values to market prices is uniform within a taxing jurisdiction, the effective tax rate will be the same on all properties. The constitutions of most states require the assessment of property at a uniform percentage of market value, often 100 percent, but in only a small minority of jurisdictions do assessments approach the level prescribed by state law. A few states authorize the assessment of various classes of property at different fractions of market value, thus subjecting each class of property to a different effective rate of tax.[13] But all jurisdictions are legally bound to assess all property within a given class at a uniform fraction of market value.

Whatever limits such facts of life place on the uniformity of prop-

11. Some states simply apply their own rates to taxable income as defined under federal law (usually with minor adjustments in such items as interest on state and federal securities). A few, such as Massachusetts and New Hampshire, employ drastically different bases.

In 1971, depending on the state they lived in, a family of four with adjusted gross income of $10,000 ($25,000) would have paid income taxes from a low of 0.5 percent (1.4 percent) to a high of 4.7 percent (6.4 percent). Advisory Commission on Intergovernmental Relations, *Federal-State-Local Finances: Significant Features of Fiscal Federalism* (1974), p. 260.

12. In 1973, three states imposed state sales taxes at rates below 3 percent, but permitted additional local taxes that brought the combined rate over 3 percent. The highest state rate was 6.5 percent in Connecticut. Alabama and New York imposed a 4 percent state rate and permitted a local add-on of up to 3 percent. Ibid., p. 238.

13. Whether the property tax rate should vary according to class of property is discussed in chap. 4.

erty taxation, actual administration falls far short of both the ideal and the achievable. The most commonly used index of nonuniformity is the "coefficient of intra-area dispersion." This statistic is equal to the average percentage difference between the assessment-sales ratio of each property and the median assessment-sales ratio in the jurisdiction.[14] It is not the only possible measure,[15] but, as the one most commonly reported in ratio studies, it will be used here.

Official statistics suggest that property tax administration in the United States, as measured by coefficients of dispersion, improved sharply between 1956 and 1966, but not since then, as indicated in table 2-4. This table refers only to single-family nonfarm housing, the class of property regarded as easiest to appraise accurately, and represents about 48 percent of assessed value. For reasons that are not altogether clear, coefficients of dispersion of less than 10 are regarded as signs of administrative excellence while those between 10 and 20 indicate acceptable administration.[16] Roughly half of all jurisdictions had "acceptable" administration by these standards in 1971, though only one in sixteen (and even fewer of large jurisdictions) had "excellent" administration. At the other extreme, large

14. For example, consider a jurisdiction in which there are eleven properties with ratios of assessed to market value of 0.1, 0.2, 0.3, . . . , 1.1. The median ratio is 0.6. The average absolute deviation is $[2(0.5) + 2(0.4) + 2(0.3) + 2(0.2) + 2(0.1)] / 11 = 0.2727$. . . . The ratio of this deviation to the median ratio, 0.6, is 0.2727 . . . $/0.6 \cong 0.45$. In this calculation, properties may be weighted equally, by market value, or in some other way. One analyst has argued that calculations based on the ratio of sales prices to assessments have statistical properties superior to those based on the reverse ratio. See Pao Lun Cheng, "The Common Level of Assessment in Property Taxation," *National Tax Journal*, vol. 23 (March 1970), pp. 50–65.

15. A general measure of distortion, D, is given by

$$D = [\Sigma (V_i)^w / n]^{\frac{1}{w}} / \overline{V},$$

where V_i is the deviation of each assessment ratio around the average $\overline{V}$, w is the weight attached to each deviation, and n is the number of observations. The parameter, w, expresses the intensity of aversion to mistakes; the larger is w, the greater is the relative weight attached to relatively big mistakes. For the coefficient of dispersion, $w = 1$. For the coefficient of variation, an index commonly used in statistics, $w = 2$. In principle, w can be any positive number. Note that the coefficient of dispersion is based on deviations around the median, not the average, an inferior procedure. See note 17 below.

16. In fact, the standard of administrative excellence should take account of the difficulty of accurately assessing properties within the jurisdiction, which depends on the rate of change of property values, the number of sales, and numerous other factors. See app. B.

Table 2-4. Distribution of Assessing Jurisdictions by Coefficient of Dispersion, Single-Family Nonfarm Houses, Selected Years, 1956–71

Percent

Coefficient of dispersion	All areas				Areas with population of 50,000 or more			
	1956	1961	1966	1971	1956	1961	1966	1971
0–9.9	}7.9	2.9	7.6	6.7	}5.1	1.8	4.4	3.7
10.0–14.9		10.8	20.6	17.9		10.1	25.8	19.0
15.0–19.9	12.5	16.2	25.2	24.3	15.9	20.9	30.6	29.4
20.0–24.9	15.1	17.7	15.7	18.1	17.0	24.7	15.9	20.2
25.0–29.9	14.6	14.3	11.3	12.1	19.0	17.6	11.3	12.1
30.0–39.9	21.2	18.7	9.8	11.8	22.5	17.8	6.7	10.0
40.0–49.9	11.6	8.8	5.5	5.2	9.9	5.3	3.5	3.9
50.0 or more	17.1	10.6	4.3	3.9	10.6	1.8	1.8	1.7
Total	100.0	100.0	100.0	100.0	100.0	100.0	100.0	100.0

Sources: U.S. Bureau of the Census, *Census of Governments, 1972*, vol. 2, *Taxable Property Values and Assessment-Sales Price Ratios*, pt. 2, *Assessment-Sales Price Ratios and Tax Rates* (1973), table J, p. 14; and Bureau of the Census, *Census of Governments*, vol. 5, *Taxable Property Values in the United States* (1969), table 16, p. 84. Details may not add to totals because of rounding.

numbers of jurisdictions had atrocious administration, as measured by coefficients of dispersion. One jurisdiction in eleven exhibited coefficients over 40.[17]

Since administrative inaccuracy has greater consequences when tax rates are high than when they are low, it is reassuring that jurisdictions with high property taxes tend to administer them somewhat more equitably than do jurisdictions with low tax rates. On the average an increase in property taxes of $100 per property per year

17. First prize in 1971 should be awarded to Warren County, Kentucky, with a coefficient of dispersion of 1.1. Booby prize would go to Washington County, Pennsylvania, with a coefficient of 85.2. If appraisals as a fraction of market value fall in a rectangular distribution, the coefficient of dispersion tends toward 50 for numbers of properties found even in small towns. For example, with twenty properties the coefficient of dispersion is 0.48. Since one would expect ratios of assessed to market values to cluster around the average, coefficients of dispersion larger than 0.5 seem to require awe-inspiring incompetence or malice. Such is not the case, however. Because the coefficient of dispersion is based on deviations from median, not average, ratios, it has no maximum value. Take a town with three properties, two assessed at $100k$ percent of value, the other at $100m$ percent of value. The coefficient of dispersion, then, is $(m - k)/3k$, which may take on any positive value, because m is unbounded from above. This example suggests that high values of coefficients of dispersion are due to skewed distributions of assessment-sales ratios. It also suggests a major inadequacy in the measure since it is not an index of the misallocation of tax burdens among taxpayers. Such an indicator would have to be based on deviations of assessment-sales ratios from the average (not the median) in the district.

is associated with a statistically significant (if surprisingly small) reduction in the coefficient of dispersion by 1 point.[18] Thus, the predicted coefficient of dispersion is 21.4 when the average property tax is $300 and 18.5 when the average property tax is $600.

Conclusion

The label "property tax" covers a bewildering variety of taxes levied at different rates according to different rules on different tax bases. One way of defining the characteristics of a tax is by the amounts people must pay at a particular time and by the changes in tax liabilities that various events or actions will produce. Viewed in this light the property tax varies widely in amount for households in similar circumstances and, perhaps more important, it changes by widely varying amounts as property values change. Thus, the incentives to acquire or to improve real property differ among jurisdictions. These incentives are central to an understanding of how the burdens of the property tax are distributed among households in the United States, the issue to which chapter 3 is addressed.

18. A regression of the coefficient of dispersion, *CD*, on the average property tax on single-family homes, *APT* (calculated as the median effective rate on fully taxable single-family homes times mean assessed value divided by the ratio of assessed to market values), is

$$CD = 24.32 - 0.0097 APT.$$
$$(-5.69)$$
$$\bar{R}^2 = 0.082; \ N = 354.$$

(Here and in following expressions the numbers in parentheses are *t*-values.) The observations are cities with populations of 50,000 or more surveyed in the 1972 Census of Governments. See vol. 2, pt. 2, *Assessment–Sales Price Ratios and Tax Rates*, pp. 60–103.

CHAPTER THREE

Incidence
of the Property Tax

IN A NAIVE SENSE, the answer to the question in the title of this volume is obvious: property owners pay property taxes. The more important question concerns how property taxes change the behavior of owners and how such responses alter the real incomes of all families. To the extent that property owners can change their receipts (by raising rents, for example), they may be able to shift tax burdens to others.

In fact, the answer to the title's question depends on the scale of the envisioned change. For example, voters in Maryland counties may consider the replacement of part of the property tax by some other revenue source when they decide whether to exercise the option the state gives them to levy a surcharge of up to 50 percent of the state income tax collected from county residents. The higher the surcharge, the lower are the property taxes required to finance a given amount of county expenditures. Voters of all states make similar choices when they alter formulas for state aid for locally financed public education. In all these cases, voters decide the proportions of more or less independently determined state or local expenditures that will be financed from property taxes and from other state or local revenues. In doing so, they—and the legislators they elect—want to know who will gain and who will lose.

People also want to know who will gain and who will lose from

national policies that will reduce or increase property taxes across
the nation. Who has borne the brunt of the increase in the proportion of gross national product claimed by property taxes, and how
would those burdens change if, say, income or sales taxes were
raised, and property taxes lowered?

Both of these questions concern the substitution of one tax for
another, or "differential tax incidence." Economic analysis of differential tax incidence has undergone massive revision in the last
decade. As a result, opinions among economists engaged in the
study of tax incidence bear little resemblance to views generally
held even a few years ago. The main contribution of recent research
has been to show that the pattern of gains and losses generated when
a single state or locality changes property taxes will differ markedly
from that appearing after a change in the nationwide use of property taxes, and that none of these patterns resembles the profile of
burdens from property taxes that economists formerly described.
Popular discussions of the property tax and proposals to amend it,
on the other hand, have been carried on without regard for the
new analysis. This oversight is normal—it takes time for academic
advances to filter into popular debate—and frequently would cause
no concern; but in this case, the implications for public policy of
the new analysis are radically different from those of the old, and
important modifications in property taxation are now under discussion.

The change in viewpoint may be summarized as follows. Under
the old view no distinction usually was drawn between changes in
property taxes within a single locality and changes in the nation.[1]
The real property tax was treated as a tax on land and structures
that causes increases in the prices of goods and services produced
with the tax base. The burden of the property tax on structures was
felt to be borne in proportion to *consumption* of such commodities.
Following this logic, the tax was regressive, because consumption
(especially of housing, in whose price the property tax is an especially large component) looms larger in the budgets of low-income

1. "Locality," as used here, refers to any part of the United States sufficiently
small so that changes in local policy have negligible effects on the supply of capital
to other regions. A locality, in this sense, may be a city, a county, a state, or even
a group of small states. By contrast, some metropolitan areas—New York, for
example—are too large to be classed as a locality.

families than of those of the well-to-do. The tax on land was alleged to be borne by landowners, and this component was seen as progressive.

Under the new view, this approach is roughly correct for analyzing the distributional effects of changes in property taxes by a given locality, but not in the nation as a whole. In the latter case the property tax is viewed as an element in the cost of using taxed *capital* goods, including land. Since not all capital goods are taxed, investors will shift resources from heavily to lightly taxed (or untaxed) activities. Through these adjustments the rate of return to all owners of capital goods, even those not directly subject to property taxation, will be reduced. Under plausible assumptions, all owners of capital share the burden of the property tax. In this case, it is a progressive tax, since ownership of capital is even more concentrated among high-income families than is income.

Under the old view the property tax is a foe of egalitarian goals; under the new, a friend. This chapter will set forth both views in some detail and review the criticisms to which each is subject. Most of the available evidence supports the new view and suggests, therefore, that many current proposals for changes in the property tax rest on misconceptions about its impact on the distribution of income.[2]

The Traditional View

Until recently, analysis of the burdens of the property tax rested on the simple theory of supply and demand taught in introductory courses in economics. For this purpose the property tax was divided into two parts.

The Tax on Land

The tax on land was borne by landowners because of the well-established proposition that any tax levied on a commodity in fixed

2. Under both the old and the new views, the effects on income distribution of an equal change in local expenditures and property taxes may be quite different from the effects of replacing one tax with another—the effects examined here. In the former case, local property taxes serve as the price for local governmental services. Taxes imposed on a particular class of property do not, in general, equal the value of services consumed by its occupants. If the value of services differs property taxes, one would expect the selling price of such properties to reflect this fiscal residual. This process will be examined in chap. 4.

supply will be borne by owners of that commodity as demonstrated by the diagram below. The value of that commodity to its users, p_0,

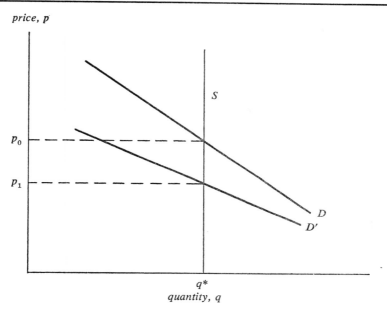

price, p

p_0

p_1

S

D

D'

q^*

quantity, q

An ad valorem tax reduces the net proceeds accruing to suppliers of any product in fixed supply, S, and may be regarded as a reduction in the demand curve faced by suppliers from D to D'. Demanders offer p_0 per unit when q^* units are supplied, but suppliers receive only p_1, with the difference, $p_0 - p_1$, accruing to the tax collector. Since suppliers offer the same quantity, q^*, regardless of the price, and demanders offer p_0 per unit when q^* units are offered, suppliers suffer the entire tax burden. At any higher (lower) gross price than p_0, excess supply (demand) will prevail.

is unaffected by the tax. Hence, the price that they will pay for the fixed quantity, q^*, of the taxed commodity is unaffected. If the ownership of the taxed commodity is widely diffused, no owner will be able successfully to raise his price, as all his customers will desert him. Even if ownership is concentrated and owners collude to maximize joint profits, the level of property taxes will not affect the maximizing price, and hence will not cause owners to alter land prices.[3]

3. Let t be the ad valorem property tax rate, p the unit price of land, $q = f(p)$ the quantity of land demanded, and r the total economic rent of all land. The as-

As a result, they bear the tax. The only circumstance under which property taxes on land might be shifted to users would be if land ownership were highly concentrated, if prices were below the level at which profits could be maximized, and if owners used an increase in property taxes as a signal to raise prices. In fact, however, land ownership is widely diffused in virtually all urban areas, so that the competitive model is the relevant one nearly everywhere. The conclusion that the property tax on land is borne by owners is indisputable as long as the supply of land is regarded as fixed.[4]

The question is, "Which owners?" A simple example will illustrate the problem. A man owns land that rents for $1,000 per year and (assuming that the prevailing yield on land is 10 percent) is worth $10,000. He wishes to sell. Just before sale, the land becomes subject to property taxes of $400 per year. As a result, the value of the land declines to $6,000, since the value of the net income of $600 ($1,000 less the $400 tax) capitalized at 10 percent is $6,000. The sale is then completed. Who bears the tax? Clearly, the original owner did, since it reduced the value of his land. The new landowner legally pays the tax, but bears no economic burden. He received an asset yielding $600, for which he paid the going price of $6,000; his net worth was unaffected by the tax.[5]

The foregoing example points up the serious difficulties in estimating empirically the distribution of burdens of property taxes on land. Present landowners bear only those increases in the property tax rate that have been imposed since they purchased the property. If they acquired the land by bequest or gift, they bear that portion of the increase imposed since the land was last sold. The part of the rate imposed before current owners purchased the property is borne

---

sumption that the cost of supplying land is zero implies that all costs of improving the land itself (for instance, grading, sewage connections) are treated as sunk costs. By definition $r = (1 - t) [p \cdot f(p)]$, and $dr/dp = (1 - t) [pf'(p) + f(p)] = 0$ is the first-order condition for maximizing profits. Since $(1 - t)$ cancels out, the price at which net profits are maximized is independent of the tax rate. In other words, profits are maximized when the marginal revenue from a cut in prices is zero. The tax does not affect the price at which this occurs.

4. On variability in the supply of land to taxing jurisdictions, see chap. 5.

5. In fact, the problem would be much more complicated if tax increases were anticipated. For an excellent analysis of the consequences of capitalization, see Bruce W. Hamilton, "Capitalization of Intra-Jurisdictional Differences in Local Tax Prices" (Johns Hopkins University, no date; processed).

by previous owners, their heirs, or recipients of their gifts who may or may not be landowners at present. For these reasons it is incorrect to allocate the burden of property taxes on land according to the present ownership. Nevertheless, most analysts have made this assumption, although it would be preferable to allocate land taxes in proportion to ownership of capital.

The Tax on Structures

Until recently, analysis of the incidence of property taxes on structures differed from that on land primarily because the supply of structures was not regarded as fixed (see the diagram below). Ac-

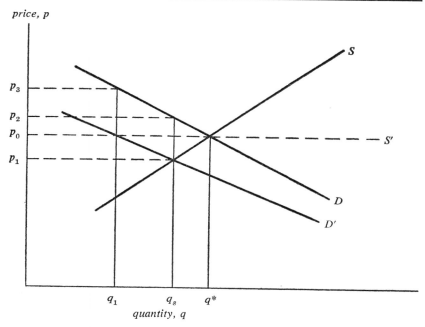

The supply of the product varies with price along S in the short run. The tax reduces demand from D to D' and causes prices received by suppliers to fall by $p_0 - p_1$ and that paid by demanders to rise by $p_2 - p_0$. The quantity demanded falls to q_s in the short run. If, with the passage of time, the supply of the service or commodity is completely elastic—that is, none of the service or commodity will be supplied at a price permanently below p_0 and any amount demanded will be supplied at that price—demanders pay the tax in full through an increase in the price by the amount $p_3 - p_0$, the amount of the tax, and the quantity demanded, D', declines to q_1.

cording to the traditional view, any amount of capital for improvements in real property is available in the long run at a fixed cost determined by the productivity of capital in other uses. Although variability in the supply of structures is only partial in the short run, users of real property eventually must pay property taxes on structures through higher sales prices or rents (imputed rents, in the case of owner-occupants). After sufficient time, an increase in property taxes will shrink the stock of structures and force up their rental prices. The process begins much like that triggered by a tax on land. A rise in taxes would initially fall on owners, reducing their net income. Either of two sets of events might ensue. In the first, owners, now denied their former rates of return on investment in structures, may curtail investment in new structures, rehabilitation, and maintenance. As a result, the stock of structures will become less valuable than the stock that would have prevailed in the absence of the tax; and users will pay higher rents for the restricted stock. This process will continue until the rental income per dollar of new construction, *net of tax*, is as high as it was before taxes were increased. Rents will therefore be increased by the amount of the tax. Alternatively, owners may short-circuit this process by raising rents directly when taxes increase. This course is more likely if demand for structures is rising independently—for example, because of population growth. In that case the increase in prices induced by higher taxes causes demand for structures to rise less than it otherwise would have. The end result is the same as in the first case.

Regardless of the mechanism, the rent on structures, after all adjustments have taken place, equals the rental cost of the capital embodied in them (which equals the sum of interest on the value of the structure, depreciation, and maintenance, less anticipated capital gains, none of which are affected directly by property taxes) plus property taxes. The same analysis applies to tax cuts.[6]

Because structures must be renewed periodically, the property tax they bear, according to this view, is not capitalized. The price of structures, exclusive of taxes, is determined, rather, by construction and maintenance costs. Furthermore, the tax is simply an element of the gross cost of the structure to users.

This theory of tax incidence suggests that families bear property

---

6. The role of corporation income and personal income taxes will be treated below.

taxes (except those on land) in proportion to their purchases of goods and services produced by taxed structures. Property taxes on residential structures would be borne in proportion to housing expenditures, actual or imputed.[7] Part of the price of all other goods would consist of property taxes on structures, used directly or indirectly in the production of such goods.[8] Ignoring the fact that the menu of goods purchased by each family differs and that the proportion of costs of various commodities represented by structures also differs, one can allocate the burden of property taxes on nonresidential structures in proportion to family consumption and the burden of residential property taxes according to housing expenditures, actual and imputed. This rule of thumb, or something close to it, has been followed by most empirical studies of tax incidence based on the traditional view of property taxes. Because the ratio of consumption to income diminishes as income rises, so does the ratio of property tax burdens to income under this view—that is, the property tax is regressive.

Estimated Tax Burdens: The Traditional View

Empirical estimates of the distribution of burdens built upon the analysis just set forth invariably show the property tax to be regressive. Table 3-1 reports four such estimates, all prepared within the last decade. The results differ in detail because they refer to different years, employ different income concepts, embody slightly different assumptions about shifting, and cover different parts of the property tax. Despite these differences, they agree in depicting the property tax as regressive with respect to measured income, although the degree of regression for the tax on owner-occupied housing as reported by the Advisory Commission on Intergovernmental Relations far exceeds that calculated for the entire property tax by Pechman and Okner, the Musgraves, and Netzer.[9] As noted above,

7. Actually, tax burdens would be proportional to housing expenditures only if the ratio of structural value to land value is uniform and rent-value ratios were constant across income classes.

8. Structures enter indirectly into the production of good *A* if, for example, they are used directly in producing good *B*, which is then used to produce good *A*.

9. The range of burdens estimated by Pechman and Okner is wider than that of the Musgraves primarily because the former distinguish very high income brackets. Their estimated burden for the top decile is 2.9 percent, roughly in accord with estimates of the Musgraves. See Joseph A. Pechman and Benjamin A. Okner, *Who Bears the Tax Burden?* (Brookings Institution, 1974), table 4-9, variant 3b, p. 161.

Table 3-1. Estimates of the Property Tax as a Percentage of Income under the Traditional View, by Income Class, Various Years, 1957–70

Income classes in thousands of dollars; other figures in percent

	Netzer—1957			Musgraves—1968		Pechman-Okner—1966		ACIR[a]—1970	
	Money income class[b]	Nonresidential property	Residential property	Total property	Income class[b]	Total property	Family income class[b]	Total property	Family income class[b]	Residential property[c]
	Less than 2	4.0	3.3	7.3	Less than 4	6.7	Less than 3	6.5	Less than 2	16.6
	2-3	3.4	1.6	5.0	4.0-5.7	5.7	3-5	4.8	2-3	9.7
	3-4	3.2	1.4	4.6	5.7-7.9	4.7	5-10	3.6	3-4	7.7
	4-5	3.4	1.4	4.8	7.9-10.4	4.3	10-15	3.2	4-5	6.4
	5-7	2.2	1.7	3.9	10.4-12.5	4.0	15-20	3.2	5-6	5.5
	7-10	1.6	2.0	3.6	12.5-17.5	3.7	20-25	3.1	6-7	4.7
	10-15	1.3	2.7	4.0	17.5-22.6	3.3	25-30	3.1	7-10	4.2
	15 and over	1.7	1.6	3.3	22.6-35.5	3.0	30-50	3.0	10-15	3.7
					35.5-92.0	2.9	50-100	2.8	15-25	3.3
					92.0 and over	3.3	100-500	2.4	25 and over	2.9
							500-1,000	1.7		
							1,000 and over	0.8		
Average, all classes		...	...	4.6	Average, all classes	3.9	Average, all classes	3.4	Average, all classes	4.9

Sources: Dick Netzer, Economics of the Property Tax (Brookings Institution, 1966), table 3-3, p. 45, and table 3-10, p. 55; Richard A. Musgrave and Peggy B. Musgrave, Public Finance in Theory and Practice (McGraw-Hill, 1973), p. 368; Joseph A. Pechman and Benjamin A. Okner, Who Bears the Tax Burden? (Brookings Institution, 1974), table 4-8, variant 3b, p. 59; Advisory Commission on Intergovernmental Relations, Financing Schools and Property Tax Relief—A State Responsibility (ACIR, 1973), table 15, p. 36.
The assumptions about shifting are as follows:

Netzer: The tax on owner-occupied single-family structures is borne by occupants; the tax on rental and owner-occupied multifamily structures is borne in proportion to rent paid; the tax on residential land is borne in proportion to rental income; the nonresidential property tax is partly shifted forward, partly borne by owners.

Musgraves: The tax on owner-occupied housing is borne by owners; the tax on rental housing is borne by tenants in proportion to rent; the tax on other property is borne half by consumers in proportion to consumption outlays, and half by all asset holders in proportion to capital income.

Pechman-Okner: The tax on land is borne by landowners; the tax on all structures is borne in proportion to housing expenditures and consumption.

a. Advisory Commission on Intergovernmental Relations.

b. The income concepts used by the various studies are as follows:

Netzer: Money income.

Musgraves: Money factor income, employee wage supplements, imputed rent, interest on life insurance, transfers, corporation profits minus dividends, other accrued asset gains.

Pechman-Okner: Wages, salaries, interest, dividends, rents and royalties, transfer payments, capital gains accrued during the year, and indirect business taxes.

ACIR: Money wages or salaries; net income from farm self-employment; social security benefits; dividends, interest (on savings or bonds), income from estates or trusts or net rental income; public assistance or welfare payments; unemployment compensation, government employee pensions or veterans' benefits; private pensions, annuities, alimony, regular contributions from persons not living in the household, net royalties, and other periodic income.

c. Owner-occupied single-family houses.

similar patterns appear because property taxes are assumed to be roughly proportional to consumption (especially housing expenditures) which, as a percentage of measured income, declines as income rises. None of the authors of these estimates adheres rigidly to the distribution of burdens shown in the table. The Musgraves list a number of alternative ways of distributing property taxes, but exclude them from their estimates of overall budget incidence. Netzer has recently acknowledged many of the shortcomings of the estimates cited here and concludes that the property tax, on balance, is probably progressive.[10] Pechman and Okner present distributions based on all major theories of tax incidence without expressing a preference among them. Nevertheless, these distributions are so firmly embedded in the perceptions of the property tax held by the public and much of the economics profession that a detailed criticism is in order.

Criticisms of Estimated Burdens

The estimates presented in table 3-1 are subject to a number of criticisms.[11] Some, such as the failure to consider the wide variations in tax rates across jurisdictions, are acknowledged by their authors and are inevitable because of aggregation or lack of data. Others involve the theory of tax incidence on which the estimates rest and will be examined below.

THE ACCOUNTING PERIOD. In virtually all studies of tax incidence, families are classified on the basis of measured *annual* income,[12] solely because official statistics are collected that way. In principle, families could be classified by monthly, weekly, or daily income. The year is used because incomes vary in the short run for reasons unrelated to basic economic circumstances. As an extreme example, if families were classified on the basis of weekly incomes, those whose

10. Dick Netzer, "The Incidence of the Property Tax Revisited," *National Tax Journal*, vol. 26 (December 1973), pp. 515–35.

11. See, for example, M. Mason Gaffney, "The Property Tax is a Progressive Tax," in National Tax Association, *Proceedings of the Sixty-fourth Annual Conference on Taxation, 1971* (NTA, 1972), p. 408.

12. The definition of income may vary, as in the studies cited in table 3-1. The only conspicuous exception is Thomas Mayer, who estimates the tax burden as a percent of permanent, rather than measured, income. See his "The Distribution of Tax Burden and Permanent Income," *National Tax Journal*, vol. 27 (March 1974), pp. 141–46.

earners are paid monthly would have zero earnings in forty out of every fifty-two surveys, but would continue to spend on the basis of average weekly income. But since tax burdens customarily are based on reported consumption expenditures, massive numbers of families with "zero earnings" in the survey week would appear to suffer unconscionable tax burdens—sizable tax liabilities and no income. By contrast, families whose earners were paid in the survey period would pay property taxes equal to only a negligible part of income. The use of a very short accounting period would guarantee, therefore, that the property tax (or any other tax) would appear highly regressive, whether or not it was regressive in fact.[13]

Measurement of income over a period as long as one year eliminates most of these problems—the variations in pay periods, seasonal unemployment, Christmas bonuses, and the like—but it does not eliminate them all. Each year some workers suffer unusually lengthy illness or unemployment (while others work more or are better paid than is customary); some withdraw from the labor force to go to school or to care for children (and some enter); and some families sustain unusual business or capital losses (or gains).

The longer the period over which income is measured the less likely it is to give a misleading picture of the family's economic circumstances. In fact, the "right" period to use depends on the problem at hand. Reliance on annual income will yield approximately accurate estimates of income tax burdens faced by households at each income level, since except for loss carry-backs and carry-forwards, income averaging, and deductions related to average income over a number of years, the income tax liability of a household temporarily at one income level is no different from that of a household normally at that income level. But even under the personal income tax, provisions are made for these exceptions, because other-

---

13. Assume that forty families earn $200 per week, that one-fourth are paid each week; and that ten families earn $400 per week paid every week. Assume further that a tax accounts for 6 percent of the earnings of the $200 per week group and 10 percent of the earnings of the $400 per week—that the tax is in fact progressive. A distribution of estimated tax burdens based on income received in a given survey week would show thirty families with zero earnings paying an average of $12 in property taxes—an infinite tax rate; ten families, with earnings of $400, paying $40 in taxes—a 10 percent rate; and ten families earning $800 paying $12 in taxes—a 1.5 percent tax rate. This progressive tax seems regressive solely because of the inappropriately short accounting period.

wise a progressive income tax would fall more heavily on families with fluctuating incomes than on those with constant incomes. Many tax experts feel that the principle of averaging should be extended to the taxpayer's lifetime income.[14]

While the use of annual income, rather than average income over a longer period, does not seriously distort the income tax rate at any income level, it does affect the size distribution of income, and hence, the long-run distribution of tax burdens among income classes. Table 3-2, and the diagram appearing on page 31, compare the degree of income inequality based on a single year's income with that based on a five-year average. The diagram shows three Lorenz curves—the cumulative percentage of income received by families ordered from poorest to richest—based on data for 1967, 1971, and the average over 1967–71. Table 3-2 reports other statistics commonly used to describe the degree of inequality.

As is apparent, inequality is sharper for any single year than it is over a longer period because of the tendency for especially good and bad years to even out. Many families with low measured income in 1967 were significantly better off in later years and many with high income in 1967 were significantly worse off thereafter.

Distributions of property tax burdens are a leading example of the misleading results that annual income can give, especially when these taxes are assumed to be related to housing expenditures and to other consumption, as in table 3-1. Housing expenditures ordinarily are shaped by income averaged over a period considerably longer than one year. Neither the unlucky worker who suffers an unusual spell of unemployment or illness, nor his lucky colleague who is blessed by extra overtime or a Christmas bonus, is likely solely on that account to change his residence. Other consumption outlays also are related to income received over periods longer than one year.[15] Thus, using annual income makes the distribution of tax

14. For the best discussion of the varieties and problems of income averaging, see William Vickrey, *Agenda for Progressive Taxation* (Ronald, 1947), chap. 6.

15. On this subject the economics profession is virtually unanimous. See Milton Friedman, *A Theory of the Consumption Function* (Princeton University Press for the National Bureau of Economic Research, 1957), pp. 137–52; Franco Modigliani and Richard Brumberg, "Utility Analysis and the Consumption Function: An Interpretation of Cross Section Data," in Kenneth K. Kurihara (ed.), *Post-Keynesian Economics* (Rutgers University Press, 1954), pp. 388–436; Albert Ando and Franco Modigliani, "The 'Life Cycle' Hypothesis of Saving: Aggregate

Table 3-2. Alternative Measures of Inequality of Annual and Five-Year Average
Incomes, 1967, 1971, and 1967–71 Average

| | Annual income | | Average income, 1967–1971 |
Measure	1967	1971	
Gini coefficient[a]	0.3296	0.3511	0.3074[b] (0.2674)[c]
Log variance[d]	0.518	0.506	0.392
Proportion of population with income less than one-half of median[e]	19.1	19.2	15.7
Normalized interquartile range[f]	0.866	0.965	0.782

Source: Derived from data from University of Michigan, Survey Research Center, Panel Study of Income Dynamics.

a. The Gini coefficient is the ratio of the area between the Lorenz curve and the diagonal line to the total area below the diagonal line. See diagram, p. 31.

b. Gini coefficient of spending units arrayed from poorest to richest by their average incomes in the period 1967–71.

c. Gini coefficient of spending units arrayed by their incomes in 1967.

d. The log variance is the variance of the natural logarithm of income and is

$$\sum_{i=1}^{n} (\log Y_i - \overline{\log Y})^2/n,$$

where Y_i is income of spending unit i, $\overline{\log Y}$ is the average of the log Y_i, and n is the number of spending units.

e. Median income is the income level that divides the population of spending units on the basis of income into two groups of equal size.

f. The normalized interquartile range is the difference between the income of the spending unit at the seventy-fifth percentile and the income of the spending unit at the twenty-fifth percentile divided by the median income.

burdens appear more regressive than it would if average or "normal" income, defined over the appropriate period, were used.

Prevailing evidence suggests that the difference between the consumption-income ratios of high- and low-income families is negligible if normal income is used. Because nonresidential property taxes, under the traditional view, are assumed to be borne in proportion to consumption other than housing, this analysis of consumption behavior implies that such taxes are proportional to normal income.

Netzer has argued that policy concerning the residential property tax should be based on current income, not long-term normal income.[16] He holds that estimates of the elasticity of housing demand with respect to normal income are unreliable; that deviations of annual from normal income should *not* be ignored in setting tax policy; and that over periods longer than a year, households are increasingly likely to reside in more than one taxing jurisdiction, and accompanying variations in tax rates should be taken into ac-

Implications and Tests," *American Economic Review*, vol. 53 (March 1963), pp. 55–84; and almost any textbook in macroeconomics, such as Paul Wonnacott, *Macroeconomics* (Irwin, 1974).

16. "Incidence of the Property Tax Revisited," pp. 527–30.

percent of income

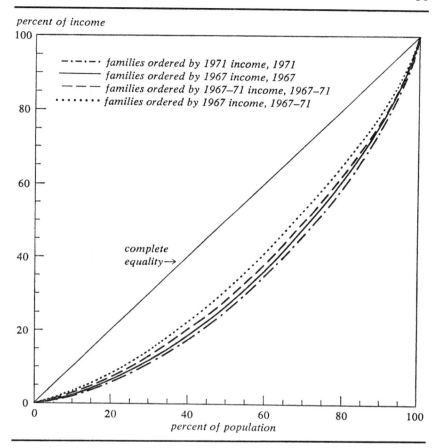

percent of population

count if normal income is used. These arguments have no bearing whatever on whether annual or normal income should be used in studies of property tax incidence.[17] They do bear directly on whether tax policy should take account of deviations of current from normal income. In general, such deviations should be recognized—as they are under the income tax—through some form of "averaging" that

17. The point simply is that normal income is superior to annual income in defining *present* economic status. If estimates of the elasticity of housing demand to annual income have varied less than permanent-income elasticities, that is no justification for being precisely wrong rather than approximately right. If the fact that people move is an argument against using normal income, the proper variable is daily, not annual, income. U.S. Bureau of the Census, *Current Population Reports*, series P-20, no. 188, "Mobility of the Population of the United States, March 1967 to March 1968" (1969), table 1.

allows taxpayers to adjust tax liabilities during years of unusual income.[18]

If the residential property tax is distributed in proportion to housing consumption, then, subject to a qualification presented in the next section, it is progressive, proportional, or regressive with respect to normal income as housing expenditures are distributed progressively, proportionally, or regressively with respect to normal income. The published evidence on housing demand is mixed, but housing consumption seems to be roughly proportional to normal income.[19]

THE VALUE-RENT RATIO AND THE EFFECTIVE TAX RATE. In the United States the property tax on rental housing is imposed on the gross value of the property, not on the amount of rents collected. If property taxes are shifted to tenants, as assumed in the distributions reported in table 3-1, the pattern of burdens should depend not only on the ratio of rental expenditures to income for different income classes, but also on the ratio of property values to rents of housing occupied by tenants at different income levels and on the ratio of taxes to market values.

The tax burden on a renter (if he bears the tax) as a fraction of income is simply

$$(1) \qquad T/Y = (T/V) \ (V/R) \ (R/Y),$$

where T is the tax levied on a rental unit with rent R and value V, and Y is income.

Little evidence is available on the correlation between value-rent ratios (V/R) and effective tax rates (T/V) on the one hand, and tenant income on the other. Peterson has presented evidence that

18. This issue is addressed at greater length in chap. 5.
19. See Frank de Leeuw, "The Demand for Housing: A Review of Cross-Section Evidence," *Review of Economics and Statistics*, vol. 53 (February 1971), pp. 1–10; Henry J. Aaron, *Shelter and Subsidies: Who Benefits From Federal Housing Policies?* (Brookings Institution, 1972), app. C. For some evidence that the income elasticity of housing demand is below 1—that is, that the proportion of normal income spent on housing declines with income—see Geoffrey Carliner, "Income Elasticity of Housing Demand," *Review of Economics and Statistics*, vol. 55 (November 1973), pp. 528–32, and Sherman J. Maisel, James B. Burnham, and John S. Austin, "The Demand for Housing: A Comment," *Review of Economics and Statistics*, vol. 53 (November 1971), pp. 410–13. See also, Elizabeth Roistacher, "Housing and Homeownership," in James N. Morgan (ed.), *Five Thousand American Families—Patterns of Economic Progress*, vol. 2, *Special Studies of the First Five Years of the Panel Study of Income Dynamics* (University of Michigan, Survey Research Center, 1974), pp. 1–40.

value-rent ratios increased sharply with market rent in selected cities.[20] This phenomenon reflects the typical location of inexpensive rental housing in older buildings with relatively short expected lives and relatively high maintenance and insurance costs. In addition, new buildings with higher rents tend to be in urban fringes where land values are appreciating, while older buildings are often located where land values are declining;[21] as a result owners of high-rent units tend to realize more of their profits through capital gains than do owners of low-rent units, further increasing the disparity of value-rent ratios. Peterson reports value-rent ratios ranging from three or four on very low-rent housing to ten or more on more costly rental units.[22] Stegman reports value-rent ratios of two or less in central Baltimore.[23] Unfortunately, Peterson's and Stegman's results refer to only a handful of cities; furthermore, Netzer notes that aggregative data from the Census of Housing do not support the findings that value-rent ratios rise with rent paid.[24] He speculates that Peterson's results may apply to comparisons between value-rent ratios on rented housing of relatively low quality and on moderate-priced housing, particularly in large urban areas, and that value-rent ratios on moderate and expensive rental housing may differ negligibly.

The significance of variations in value-rent ratios is undercut to the extent that faulty property tax administration raises (lowers) tax burdens on low- (high-) priced housing. Such a pattern may develop because of lags in reassessment; in that event, properties that are appreciating more rapidly (or depreciating less rapidly) than average are persistently undervalued, while overvaluation is the fate of properties appreciating less rapidly (or depreciating more

20. George E. Peterson, "The Regressivity of the Residential Property Tax," Working Paper 1207-10 (Urban Institute, 1972).

21. There is some evidence that new structures may actually appreciate during the first year after construction, perhaps because they must pass through an expensive shakedown period or because uncertainty regarding the eventual vacancy level and the character of tenants causes investors to discount their value at first. See Frank C. Wykoff, "Evaluation of the Depreciation Allowances for Real Property" (Pomona College, July 1973; processed).

22. The elasticity of the value-rent ratio to rent is 0.5 to 0.7.

23. See Michael A. Stegman, *Housing Investment in the Inner City: The Dynamics of Decline: A Study of Baltimore, Maryland, 1968–1970* (MIT Press, 1972), p. 169.

24. See Netzer, "Incidence of the Property Tax Revisited," pp. 530–31.

rapidly) than average.[25] How taxes on rental property move with respect to family income is not clear. Some evidence suggests that tax rates in general diminish as property values rise. The Census Bureau finds that more than 40 percent of all jurisdictions assess low-value single-family residences at higher rates than they do high-value residences, while only 2 percent exhibit the reverse pattern.[26] In 1971, eighteen of the twenty-five largest metropolitan areas assessed multifamily dwellings at a higher proportion of market value than they did single-family dwellings.[27] To the extent that tenants bear the property tax as assumed in table 3-1 and that they have lower incomes than homeowners, such administrative practices would offset the impact of differential rent-value ratios on multi-family housing and introduce regressivity between tenants and homeowners.

Alternative Estimates of the Burden

If residential property taxes are borne by occupants, as the traditional view holds, it is possible to determine whether the tax is regressive, proportional, or progressive through statistical procedures that are free of the faults just described. The distributional pattern of a tax is given by the elasticity of tax collections with respect to normal income, $E_{T,Y}$. This statistic measures the percentage increase

25. If the ratio of assessed to true market values of two classes of properties is unequal, the class assessed at the larger fraction of market value bears more than its fair share of total property taxes. For example, if class A property is assessed at 62 percent of market value because it has appreciated 10 percent per year for five years since the last reassessment, while class B property is assessed at market value because its value has not changed in that time, class B property will pay 23.4 percent more than its fair share of taxes if class A property represents half of the tax base. If class B property represents only one-fifth of the tax base, it bears 43.7 percent more than its fair share. In general, the "exploitation" of slowly appreciating or depreciating property is greater the smaller the proportion of the tax base it represents, the greater the disparity in rates of appreciation, and the longer the period between reassessments.

26. U.S. Bureau of the Census, *Census of Governments, 1972*, vol. 2, *Taxable Property Values and Assessment–Sales Price Ratios*, pt. 2: *Assessment–Sales Price Ratios and Tax Rates* (1973), p. 15. The text statement is based on the distribution of the variable D, calculated for each jurisdiction, where $D = [(1/n)\Sigma(A_i/P_i)]/(\Sigma A_i/\Sigma P_i)$; A_i and P_i are the assessed value and price for each house, and n is the number of properties. The variable D tends to exceed 1.00 if assessment-sales ratios decline with home value. Forty percent of all jurisdictions had values of D above 1.05; 2 percent had values below 0.95.

27. Based on unpublished tabulations from the 1972 Census of Governments; see table 4-1 below.

in tax payments when income increases 1 percent. When $E_{T,Y}$ exceeds 1, a tax is progressive; when it is less than 1, a tax is regressive; when it equals 1, a tax is proportional. Using equation (1), one can show that $E_{T,Y}$ depends on three other elasticities: the elasticity of property tax rates with respect to normal income, $E_{t,Y}$ (which answers the question whether tax rates are higher or lower for poor than for wealthy taxpayers); the elasticity of housing expenditures—rents or home values—with respect to normal income, $E_{R,Y}$ (do housing expenditures as a fraction of income rise or fall with increases in income?), and the elasticity of the value-rent ratio with respect to rents, $E_{V/R,R}$.[28] If the property tax were equitably administered, so that per capita incomes and property tax rates were unrelated (that is, if $E_{t,Y} = 0$), the property tax would be progressive if the fraction of income devoted to housing expenditures rose with income (that is, if $E_{R,Y} > 1$) and if $E_{V/R}$ is not negative. Table 3-3 reports the results of one attempt to estimate $E_{T,Y}$ in a manner free from the shortcomings of the estimates reported in table 3-1 on the assumption that $E_{t,Y} = 0$.

Table 3-3 is based on a sample of households that have moved within the last year (renters) or two (homeowners), drawn from the University of Michigan's Panel Study of Income Dynamics for the years 1967–71. Information on effective property tax rates by county and cities of 50,000 or more within counties was obtained from the 1972 Census of Governments.[29] These data were matched with individual households whose county and state of residence and city size are identified in the panel study. The study also contains information on rental outlays and on market value of owner-occupied housing.

28. Let $T = (T/V)(V/R)R$, where $T =$ property taxes, $V =$ value of a rental unit with rent, R, and $t = T/V$, the effective tax rate. In logarithms $\ln T = \ln t + \ln (V/R) + \ln R$. Differentiating with respect to the logarithm of normal income, Y, yields
$$E_{T,Y} \equiv d \ln T/d \ln Y = d \ln t/d \ln Y + [d \ln (V/R)/d \ln R][d \ln R/d \ln Y] + d \ln R/d \ln Y,$$
or
(A) $$E_{T,Y} = E_{t,Y} + (1 + E_{V/R,R})E_{R,Y}.$$

29. *Taxable Property Values and Assessment–Sales Price Ratios*, pt. 2, *Assessment–Sales Ratios and Tax Rates*, table 12. Median effective tax rates on fully taxable single-family housing were used for both single- and multifamily housing; unpublished data from the Federal Housing Administration were used for some counties not covered by the Bureau of the Census survey.

Table 3-3. Estimates of Relation of Home Value, Tax Rate, Property Tax Payments, and Rent to Normal Income, 1967–71 Sample Period

	Simple regression[a]		Multiple regression[a]	
Elasticity item	Coefficient	t-value	Coefficient	t-value
Homeowners				
Home value ($E_{V,Y}$)	1.132	13.7	0.995	10.4
Tax rate ($E_{t,Y}$)	0.114	1.6	0.013	0.2
Property tax payments ($E_{T,Y}$)	1.246	10.8	1.077	10.4
Renters				
Rent ($E_{R,Y}$)	0.561	10.4	0.336	5.3
Tax rate ($E_{t,Y}$)	0.009	0.1	−0.040	−0.1
Property tax payments ($E_{T,Y}$)	0.569	6.4	0.491	5.6
Property tax payments, adjusted for value-rent elasticity[b] ($E_{T,Y}$) ($E_{V/R,Y}$)	0.850–0.962		0.500–0.567	

Sources: Basic data are from the University of Michigan, Survey Research Center, Panel Study of Income Dynamics, except for the value-rent elasticity given in note b, which is drawn from George E. Peterson, "The Regressivity of the Residential Property Tax," Working Paper 1207-10 (Urban Institute, 1972). Effective property tax rates are from U.S. Bureau of the Census, *Census of Governments, 1972*, vol. 2: *Taxable Property Values and Assessment-Sales Price Ratios*, pt. 2, *Assessment-Sales Price Ratios and Tax Rates* (1973), and for counties not reported in the Census volumes, Federal Housing Administration, unpublished data.

a. Simple regression results are the coefficient b from the regression log $r = a + b$ log Y, where r is the relevant variable for 1971 and Y is normal income. Multiple regression results are the coefficients b from the regression log $r = a + b$ log $Y + \Sigma c_i$ log z_i where b and c_i are parameters and the z_i include dummy variables with significant coefficients based on whether white or nonwhite, the size of city, distance from city of 50,000 or more, census region, marital status and number of children, presence of saving equal to less than two months of income, presence of saving equal to more than two months of income, business ownership, and labor force status.

For a listing of the regressions from which these results are drawn, see app. A.

b. Computed from equation (A) in note 28 above. The value-rent elasticity is 0.5–0.7.

Normal income, Y, was defined as

$$Y = (Y_{1971} + 0.8Y_{1970} + 0.6Y_{1969} + 0.4Y_{1968} + 0.2Y_{1967})/3.$$

Thus, normal income is a weighted average of income over a five-year period.[30]

Table 3-3 contains two sets of estimates. The simple regression estimates report the relationship between home values, rents, tax rates, and property tax payments, on the one hand, and normal income, on the other, without regard for any other influences on these variables. The multiple regression estimates remove the influence of

30. An alternative definition, $Y = (Y_{1971} + Y_{1970} + Y_{1969} + Y_{1968} + Y_{1967})/5$, performed marginally less well in regressions described below. Income includes the following items: taxable income plus total transfers of all family members, the amounts saved on do-it-yourself car repairs and additions and repairs to homes, the value of free meals, home-grown food, food stamps, and other free food, the rental value of free housing and the imputed value of owner-occupied housing, the value of free help received; minus taxes, costs of child care, union dues, and the value of free help from outside the family unit; plus windfall income.

other variables, listed in the note to the table and presented in full in appendix A. The results from the simple regressions are most relevant for comparison with the patterns in table 3-1, since the latter are, in effect, simple comparisons of tax burdens by income class. None of the regressions provides any information about the effects of intrajurisdictional variations in tax rates, arising, say, from bad administration.

In the simple regression the elasticity of home value with respect to normal income slightly, but significantly, exceeds 1: the ratio of home value to income rises slightly with income.[31] Thus, property taxes on homeowners will be slightly progressive if tax rates do not decline fairly sharply with income.

In fact, on a nationwide basis average tax rates by jurisdiction rise slightly with income. Note that these calculations assume the absence of a systematic relationship between errors in assessment and income. Indeed, there is some evidence of regressive bias in tax administration within jurisdictions. The results of table 3-3, therefore, indicate only that a well-administered property tax would be slightly, but significantly, progressive on homeowners.[32]

The estimates for renters are slightly more complicated and considerably less reliable. The elasticity of rent with respect to normal income is far below one: the ratio of rent to normal income declines sharply as normal income rises. Thus, if neither property tax rates nor value-rent ratios varied systematically with income, the property tax on renters would be highly regressive (again, assuming renters bear property taxes on their dwellings). The elasticity of tax rates on rental property with respect to normal income ($E_{t,Y}$) is insignificantly different from zero, indicating that tax rates do not vary systematically with income. On the other hand, some evidence suggests that value-rent ratios increase with rent; the estimated elasticities based on Peterson's data range from 0.5 to 0.7. Given these values, the true elasticity is not the 0.569 shown in table 3-3, but

31. The results presented in table 3-3 and described below differ in some respects from other results based on the Panel Study of Income Dynamics. Roistacher, in "Housing and Homeownership," finds lower values of $E_{R,Y}$ for homeowners. More significantly, she found that $E_{R,Y}$ varied across income classes and was lower for low-income than for high-income households. These differences are due in part to differences in samples, in independent variables, and in statistical specifications.

32. This would also be true of a tax that was badly administered in a random manner across income classes.

rather 0.85 to 0.96. At these values, the property tax on renters would be slightly regressive; and once again, a regressive bias in administration within jurisdictions would make it even more so.

On balance table 3-3 suggests that even under the traditional assumptions about property tax incidence, the residential property tax is roughly proportional, with slight progressivity for homeowners offsetting slight regressivity for renters. The estimates of the relationship between housing expenditures and normal income, on which these calculations rest, are in rough accord with other estimates of the demand for housing.[33] They suggest that quite apart from objections to the theory of tax incidence underlying the traditional view of the property tax, its correct application does not sustain the conclusion that the residential property tax is regressive.

The New View

To the deceptively simple question, "Who pays the property tax?" the opening of this chapter gave a naive answer: Property owners pay the tax. The traditional view of the incidence of the property tax rejected this answer on the grounds that owners can shift the burden to those who consume the goods and services produced by the taxed property. The new view holds that *all* owners of capital bear the property tax.[34] The analysis proceeds in three stages. The first considers the distribution of burdens from a "property" tax imposed uniformly on all property—land and capital goods alike. The second considers the redistribution of burdens arising from deviations in tax rates around the average by location and industry. The third considers the impact on the aggregate supply of land and capital of changes in after-tax rents and profits.

Stage 1: A Uniform Tax

A uniform tax on the value of all land and capital goods would be borne in full by owners of capital goods since they would be un-

---

33. See note 19 above.

34. The description of the new view presented here closely follows the analysis presented by Peter M. Mieszkowski, "The Property Tax: An Excise Tax or a Profits Tax?" *Journal of Public Economics*, vol. 1 (April 1972), pp. 73–96, and Mieszkowski, "On the Theory of Tax Incidence," *Journal of Political Economy*, vol. 75 (June 1967), pp. 250–62.

able to avoid it either by shifting assets to untaxed sectors or by raising prices. The first avenue of escape is closed because all sectors are taxed equally. The second is closed because, if property owners maximize their returns, the price at which each producer of goods and services does so is unaffected by a universal tax on the value of capital assets.[35] This conclusion follows from the uniformity of the tax rate in all sectors and the assumption (to be relaxed below) that aggregate supplies of land and capital are fixed. As a result, property (capital) tax liabilities are the same wherever capital is invested and, therefore, the tax simply reduces the yield to each owner, but does not alter his profit-maximizing output or price.[36] The burden of such a tax would be distributed in proportion to the ownership of assets. It follows that a general tax on all tangible property would not affect the price of housing or of any other commodity, nor would it affect wages and salaries; it would depress after-tax profits and rents earned by owners of capital and land by the amount of the tax.

Stage 2: Variations in Tax Rates

The property tax is not a uniform tax on land and capital, as shown conclusively in chapter 2. Some land and capital goods are wholly exempt, and effective rates vary widely. The initial effects of such deviations around the average, according to the new view, follow the lines sketched out by the traditional analysis. Rates of return on taxed assets are reduced, with the largest declines associated with the highest taxes. As a result some owners of assets subject to tax will shift them to other regions or uses. In so doing, they cause a number of consequences.

CAPITAL IMPROVEMENTS. To the extent that economic activities are mobile, after-tax rates of return to similar factors of production will tend to be equalized. If one jurisdiction imposes higher property taxes than another, the achievement of equal after-tax returns implies unequal before-tax returns. The *before*-tax rate of return on taxed capital goods in the high-tax areas or uses will tend to rise

35. See note 3 above.

36. Sometimes owners of capital may be unable to maximize profits because of such external restraints as rent or price controls or public regulation of utilities. In these situations, changes in property taxes may constitute legal justification for rent or price increases.

because the departure (or failure to enter) of some capital goods will increase the scarcity value of those that remain. By contrast, investors expanding the quantity of capital assets in low-tax areas or uses will drive down before-tax rates of return. This process occurs as investors seek the highest possible rate of return net of taxes; a higher gross return must be earned in high-tax areas to yield the same net return as in low-tax areas. The process will continue until after-tax rates of return are equal—until differences in before-tax rates of return exactly offset differentials in tax rates.

LAND. The total supply of land is approximately fixed, but the demand for and the supply of land in particular jurisdictions depend on property tax policy. Demand for land is affected because land and capital are used jointly in most economic activities; consequently, the departure of capital from jurisdictions with relatively high taxes reduces the demand for land there.

If the supply is fixed, then the new view, like the traditional view, holds that land prices and rents are determined by the value to potential occupants of particular sites and are unaffected by a tax. Hence, the imposition of a tax on land values reduces net income to landowners and diverts resources to the public sector. It has no effect on the economic behavior of any group other than landowners, who will have less to spend; this effect would be offset in the aggregate by reductions in other taxes or by the greater public spending made possible by the tax on land.

The absence of effects on economic behavior of land taxes (when the supply of land is taken as fixed) explains their century-long advocacy by economists.[37] The supply of land within individual jurisdictions may not be fixed, however, because decisions about annexation or landfill may be sensitive to property taxes.

Take, for example, a city surrounded by undeveloped farmland that is worth $1,000 per acre and that is taxed by the county at 1 percent; and assume that annual net income before taxes is $100 per acre, or $90 after property taxes. If the city also taxes land at 1 percent, farms will be converted to urban uses whenever before-tax income in such uses exceed $100 per year. When urban taxes exceed rural taxes, land must earn a premium in urban uses before it will

37. See Dick Netzer, *Economics of the Property Tax* (Brookings Institution, 1966), pp. 197–212, and the references cited there.

be converted. Because the income from land tends to diminish as one moves to the periphery of a city, the greater the difference between taxes on land in urban and rural uses, the smaller the amount of land that would be available for urban uses. The intensity of land development would be affected, causing changes in aggregate land rents, wages, profits, and prices of housing and possibly other goods.[38]

The foregoing analysis applies equally when one jurisdiction taxes both farmland and developed areas but assesses farmland on the basis of current use rather than market value. In that event, development triggers revaluation for tax purposes unrelated to changes in market value.[39]

The view that the supply of land is fixed seems more appropriate for analyzing changes in land taxes imposed by cities surrounded by other developed communities—large central cities around which there is no lightly taxed "backstop" use, such as farming. In such cities increases in land taxes will be borne solely by landowners through reductions in net land rents and land values. The notion of an expandable supply of land is more relevant for surburban communities at the periphery of urban agglomerations and for isolated towns surrounded by farms. The case for land taxation on grounds of economic efficiency is not universal, but depends on the surroundings of the taxing jurisdiction and on the willingness to assess all land on the basis of current market value. Paradoxically, it seems weakest in the rapidly developing peripheral areas for which it has been more forcefully proclaimed, and strongest for areas in which development is well advanced.

OTHER EFFECTS. Movements of capital caused by variations in tax rates across jurisdictions and among industries will affect payments to other factors of production. In high-tax areas and uses, real wage rates will decline relatively,[40] because workers will have

38. Mieszkowski, "Property Tax," and Mieszkowski, "A Critical Appraisal of Land Value Taxation" (University of Houston, May 1970; processed); A. Mitchell Polinsky and Daniel L. Rubinfeld, "The Long-Run Incidence of a Residential Property Tax and Local Public Services," Working Paper 1207-29 (Urban Institute, 1974; processed).

39. For further discussion of special farmland assessments, see chap. 5.

40. Since average wages rise almost continuously, an increase in property taxes is unlikely to cause actual declines in wages. Different rates of increase in wages can bring about sizable relative differences.

fewer capital goods to work with and because owners of capital goods may try directly to curtail wages. Thus, unless labor is perfectly mobile, wages will be higher in low-tax than in high-tax regions and uses. To the extent that population patterns and occupational choices are sensitive to differences in real wages, migration and shifts in employment eventually will reduce employment in high-tax areas and expand it in low-tax areas. In the extreme case, if labor were fully mobile, relative wages would be unaffected by the tax.

The movement out of high-tax areas of transferable capital assets and, eventually, of labor as well, will depress land values and rents there (with opposite effects in the low-tax areas that receive the capital and labor). If labor and capital were fully mobile, one would expect land rents in high-tax areas to be reduced by the full amount by which local property taxes exceed the nationwide average (and to rise accordingly in areas whose tax rates are below average).

To the extent that neither land rents nor wages directly absorb above- or below-average tax rates, relative prices of products of high-tax regions or industries will tend to rise while those of low-tax regions will tend to fall. These adjustments are likely principally for goods produced and sold in local markets and not subject to national competition.

The final effects of all of these tax-induced shifts in uses and locations of capital and labor on the distribution of tax burdens cannot be calculated precisely.[41] These patterns depend on the ratio of factors used in the lightly and heavily taxed sectors; the ease with which capital, land, and labor can be substituted for each other in the production of each commodity; the mobility of factors among regions and uses that are taxed differently; the shifts in demand when relative commodity prices change; and the degree to which products of high- and low-tax regions compete with one another in

41. One reason for the lack of precision is that the theoretical foundations of the new view are incomplete. Previous analysis has dealt with models of an economy containing two sectors and two factors of production—labor and capital (for example, see Mieszkowski, "On the Theory of Tax Incidence") and of an economy containing one sector and three factors—labor, land, and capital (Mieszkowski, "Property Tax"). None has dealt with two sectors and three factors, an indispensable extension, because the property tax falls on two factors—capital and land —one of which, after a lag, is mobile between high- and low-tax jurisdictions, the other of which is spatially immobile. The results of such a model could differ in important ways from those of the studies cited here.

national markets. Clearly, the burdens of a property tax will depress average returns to owners of land and reproducible capital. In addition, variations in tax rates around the average will induce complex changes in land rents, wages, and commodity prices that would work to the disadvantage of workers, landowners, and consumers in high-tax areas and to the advantage of these groups in low-tax areas.[42] The crucial questions in calculating the burden of the property tax come down to (a) the size of the decline in the rate of return on all land and capital due to the average rate of property taxation, and (b) the distribution of excise-tax effects among wages, rents, and prices of final goods due to variations in tax rates among jurisdictions and uses.

The Return of Capital

If the property tax applied uniformly to all assets, its burden would be shared precisely in proportion to their ownership. Since tax rates vary across regions and industries, movements of capital may cause the burdens borne by its owners to exceed or fall short of total tax collections. If average after-tax incomes of owners of capital decline by more than the amount of the tax, average incomes of workers and landowners might actually increase. The opposite result is also possible. On balance, it is plausible that the effects of movements of capital on its rate of return will approximately cancel out and that income from its ownership will fall by approximately the amount of property taxes collected.[43]

EXCISE-TAX EFFECTS. Three kinds of differences in tax rates are significant for the incidence of the property tax: differences in (1)

42. The mathematical derivation of these conclusions is not presented here because it is lengthy and is readily available elsewhere. See Arnold C. Harberger, "The Incidence of the Corporation Income Tax," *Journal of Political Economy*, vol. 70 (June 1962), pp. 215–40; Mieszkowski, "On the Theory of Tax Incidence"; and John B. Shoven and John Whalley, "A General Equilibrium Calculation of the Effects of Differential Taxation of Income from Capital in the U.S.," *Journal of Public Economics,* vol. 1 (November 1972), pp. 281–321. For a nonmathematical presentation of these results, see Charles E. McLure, Jr., "A Diagrammatic Exposition of the Harberger Model with One Immobile Factor," *Journal of Political Economy*, vol. 82 (January/February 1974), pp. 56–82. These studies do not treat land and reproducible capital separately.

43. See Harberger, "Incidence of the Corporation Income Tax," pp. 228–30, for calculations indicating that, if land and capital are treated as a composite commodity, owners of that factor are likely to bear approximately all of the burden of a tax on it.

tax rates among jurisdictions within metropolitan areas; (2) average tax rates among metropolitan areas and states; and (3) tax rates on land and capital used by various industries.

Differences in tax rates within metropolitan areas are likely to be reflected primarily in land values. The reason is that a metropolitan area constitutes a set of reasonably well-connected markets for labor, housing, and most other goods and services. Consequently, property owners have limited capacity to shift deviations around average metropolitan tax rates to workers through wages or prices for housing and other goods. As a result, property taxes above (or below) average lower (or raise) the relative attractiveness of a particular location and, hence, land prices.[44] Since some tax rates are double others within the same county, the effects on land values may be sizable. Some landowners will experience increases, others decreases, but the net effect for landowners as a class will be zero. Only if it could be shown that landowners in high-tax jurisdictions tended to have systematically higher (or lower) incomes than do those in low-tax jurisdictions would these effects of differences in property taxes be relevant for estimates of incidence by income class. In the absence of such evidence, differences in property tax rates *within* metropolitan areas may be ignored in the analysis of the tax's incidence.

To the extent that markets for housing or other goods are rigidly separated, the costs or benefits of especially high or low property taxes may be shifted from landowners to consumers limited to these markets. It is alleged, for example, that the poor in general, and blacks and ethnic minorities in particular, are confined to ghettos and therefore pay higher prices for housing and other goods within some large cities. No one knows how much the prices of housing and other goods that these groups buy are further inflated by property taxes that are higher than the average.

Property tax rates also differ within and among states and regions. In general, they are lower in the South than elsewhere in the United States, and higher in urban than in rural areas. Markets for labor, housing, and other commodities produced and consumed locally do not span regions and the nation. To the extent that labor is not completely mobile, tax-induced changes in real wages may persist. In addition, real incomes of all residents may be altered by changes in

---

44. A growing literature supports the existence of this "capitalization" phenomenon within fairly large geographical areas. See chap. 4.

the prices of goods and services not subject to national competition ("local goods"), such as housing. Property taxes that are higher than average would increase the price of local goods and normally would decrease real wages.[45]

Finally, capital goods used in the production of different commodities are taxed at different rates even within jurisdictions. For example, business personal property tends to be taxed less heavily than business real property.[46] Residential real property is taxed less heavily than business real property in a majority of large metropolitan areas.[47] These differentials act like excise taxes on consumer goods. No data are available to identify the more important of these differentials.

The crucial question is whether these excise-tax effects are positively or negatively associated with family incomes. Since intrametropolitan differentials are probably capitalized into land values and the effects of intercommodity differentials are unclear, the answer hinges primarily on whether property tax rates are positively or negatively correlated with family income on a nationwide basis. Calculations reported in table 3-4 show that they are positively correlated with income across states and across metropolitan areas, reflecting the fact that the South has both low per capita income and low property taxes. Across counties within states the positive relationship is still present, but it is weaker and less consistent. The only consistent evidence of negative correlation between tax rates and income shows up for local governments within counties in New Jersey. But, as noted above, such differences are more likely to be capitalized into land values than to affect wages or prices of local goods. The relationships described in table 3-4 indicate that regional variations in property tax rates make the tax more rather than less progressive.

Estimates of Incidence Based on the New View

Table 3-5 reports two estimates of the distribution of the part of property tax burdens that results from a reduction in the average

45. Mieszkowski, in "Property Tax," presents a "peculiar" case in which a property tax raises wages and product prices while depressing land values by more than the amount of the tax. This result occurs if labor can be substituted for capital, but land must be used in fixed proportions in production, an implausible situation.
46. See chap. 5.
47. See table 4-1.

Table 3-4. Statistics from Regression of Effective Property Tax Rates on Per Capita Income, Various Levels of Government and Various Years, 1963–72[a]

Level of government and year	Number of observations	Coefficient	t-value
All states, 1971	50	1.25	3.57
All cities with population greater			
than 50,000, 1971	356	0.74	5.76
Counties within states			
California, 1972–73	58	0.81	4.13
Idaho, 1972	44	0.18	0.80
Illinois, 1970	102	0.32	3.32
Maine, 1972	16	−0.50	−0.61
Maryland, 1970	24	0.32	1.67
New Jersey, 1970	22	0.14	0.44
Ohio, 1972	88	0.31	4.34
Rhode Island, 1972	36[b]	−0.22	−0.62
Tennessee, 1963	94	0.21	2.32
Virginia, 1972	44	0.53	1.96
Wisconsin, 1972	72	0.20	2.71
Within counties in New Jersey, 1970			
Seven counties pooled	148	−0.15	−1.45
Camden	23	−0.63	−3.10
Essex	18	−0.44	−3.47
Hudson	9	−3.04	−5.74

Sources: States—Advisory Commission on Intergovernmental Relations, *Federal-State-Local Finances: Significant Features of Fiscal Federalism* (1974), p. 174.

Cities—U.S. Bureau of the Census, *Census of Governments, 1972*, vol. 2, *Taxable Property Values and Assessment-Sales Price Ratios*, pt. 2: *Assessment-Sales Price Ratios and Tax Rates* (1973), table 12.

Counties—various state and federal reports assembled by author.

Median per capita income—Bureau of the Census, *Census of Population, 1970, General Social and Economic Characteristics*, Final Report PC(1)-C1, *United States Summary*, and Final Report PC(1)-C2, *Alabama*, through PC(1)-C52, *Wyoming*.

a. The regression is $\ln R = a + b \ln Y$, where R is the effective property tax rate and Y is per capita income.

b. Includes counties and municipalities.

rate of return to all owners of capital; the two differ only in their assumption regarding the distribution of burdens from land taxes. Like those in table 3-1, these estimates are based on current measured income and, therefore, suffer from many of the same shortcomings. The distribution of burdens remains somewhat regressive in the lower and middle ranges and progressive in the upper ranges. Better measures of normal income would increase apparent progressivity, because lower income brackets always contain households whose incomes are temporarily depressed and upper income brackets households whose incomes are temporarily inflated. On balance, the part of the property tax burden borne through a reduction in capital income is distributed progressively.

Table 3-5. Alternative Estimates of Effective Property Tax Rates, by Adjusted Family Income Class, 1966

Income classes in thousands of dollars; tax rates in percent

	Assumption regarding property tax on land	
Adjusted family income class	Borne in proportion to property income in general	Borne by landowners
0–3	2.5	2.4
3–5	2.7	2.8
5–10	2.0	2.2
10–15	1.7	1.9
15–20	2.0	2.2
20–25	2.6	2.8
25–30	3.7	3.7
30–50	4.5	4.4
50–100	6.2	6.1
100–500	8.2	7.8
500–1,000	9.6	8.8
1,000 and over	10.1	8.7
All classes	3.0	3.1

Sources: Pechman and Okner, *Who Bears the Tax Burden?* table 4-8, variant 1c, p. 59, and Pechman and Okner, unpublished estimates.

These estimates ignore the fact that property taxes paid by a homeowner are deductible even though gross imputed income on his investment is not counted as part of his income.[48] Such deductibility makes a proportional or even a progressive tax regressive to homeowners since the national Treasury pays a fraction of the property tax of all taxpayers who itemize their deductions. The fraction equals the taxpayer's marginal tax rate, which rises with his income. Hence the proportion of the tax he bears declines with income from 100 percent (for homeowners who have no taxable income or who do not itemize) to 30 percent (for single homeowners with taxable incomes of $100,000 or more, or couples with $200,000 or more). This very important provision, however, is part of the personal income tax, not the property tax, and should not be confused with analysis of the incidence of the property tax.

Present information does not permit precise allocation of the burdens flowing from the excise effects of the property tax. It is con-

48. For an analysis of these income tax advantages to homeowners, see Henry Aaron, "Income Taxes and Housing," *American Economic Review*, vol. 60 (December 1970), pp. 789–806 (Brookings Reprint 193), and Aaron, *Shelter and Subsidies*, pp. 53–73.

Table 3-6. Distribution of Burden of Hypothetical Excise-Tax Effects of Property Tax, by Economic Class[a]

Economic class[b]	Average income (dollars)	Average tax burden (percent)		
		On capital	Excise-tax effect	Total[c]
A	1,000	4	−7	−2
B	5,000	7	−2	4
C	10,000	10	−1	9
D	20,000	15	1	15
E	50,000	22	1	24

Source: Derived by the method explained in app. A.
    a. The illustration is based on nine cities inhabited by people falling in one of five economic classes, which are defined by income, assets, and consumption, with the income elasticity of consumption set at approximately 0.6 and that of assets at about 1.5. Tax rates varied from 1 to 7 percent. The burden of the average tax rate is distributed in proportion to ownership of assets. The deviations around the average are assumed to act as excise taxes or subsidies on consumption. See app. A for details.
    b. See app. A, table A-2, for the asset and consumption values for the economic classes.
    c. Details may not add to total because of rounding.

ceivable, though unlikely, that such effects would significantly alter the estimates in table 3-5. To illustrate this possibility, the burden of a property tax was calculated for a hypothetical world of nine cities with wide variations in average incomes and property taxes, under the assumption that the average tax rate was distributed in proportion to net asset holdings and that deviations of tax rates in particular cities from the "world" average lead to prices for consumer goods that deviate from their average in the same direction. The illustration is described in detail in appendix A. These excise-tax effects were distributed in proportion to consumption and hence were equivalent to local sales taxes (or subsidies) on consumption. Following the results of table 3-4, the illustration incorporates the assumption that property taxes on the average are higher in high-income than in low-income communities. The results of the illustration are set forth in table 3-6.

The excise-tax effects in this example contribute qualitatively to the overall progressivity of the property tax because the illustration incorporates the positive correlation between property tax rates and average incomes. The illustration almost certainly exaggerates the quantitative importance of excise-tax effects because interregional variations in tax rates may be shifted to landowners through changed rents or to workers through changed wages, as well as to consumers through changed prices. It oversimplifies excise-tax effects because not all product prices will be affected equally. Furthermore, property tax collections that are higher than average are associated not only with revenues from other sources that are lower than average, but also with above-average state and local expenditures.[49]

Some businesses that are subject to unusually heavy (or light) property taxes, not offset by compensating local public services, will be in a position to raise (or lower) commodity prices; others will not. In general, firms that dominate national markets, or that produce only for local markets and are shielded from outside competition (such as residential builders) are best able to shift property taxes to consumers; firms subject to intensive national competition are least able to do so.[50] Since consumers distribute their expenditures among lightly and heavily taxed goods of firms well and poorly positioned to shift product prices in response to abnormally heavy (or light) property taxes, Break's conclusion regarding the importance of property taxes for consumers seems unexceptionable:

Property tax burdens on consumers, in contrast, are probably less important than commonly supposed. They are a function only of interregional and intraurban tax differentials and not of the total property tax rate; the excise tax effects generated by those tax differentials contain labor and landlord burdens which reduce the pressures making for consumer burdens; and such national consumer burdens as do exist fall not on consumers in general but only on those with relatively strong tastes for the output of the industries that are more heavily taxed than others.[51]

Stage 3: Changes in the Supply of Capital and Labor

To the extent that property taxes reduce the rate of return to owners of capital, they may alter the rate of saving and the capital stock. If the property tax results in less saving and a smaller capital stock than would prevail if the same revenues were raised by, say, a proportional income tax, total production and real wages per worker will be smaller and the rate of return to capital higher. These consequences eventually would shift the distribution of property tax burdens.

Three questions bear on the importance of these effects: (1) How large is the change in saving rates caused by a reduction in the rate of return on saving? If it is small, it need have little effect on policy-

49. See chap. 2, note 9.
50. This classification is based on George F. Break, "General Property Taxation," in *The Economics of Public Finance*, Essays by Alan S. Blinder and others (Brookings Institution, 1974).
51. Ibid., p. 165.

making. (2) How long does it take the capital stock to adjust to any change in the rate of return to capital caused by the property tax? The slower the response, the less weight these effects should have on policy, other things held constant. (3) How important are the distributional consequences or other political considerations of a decision to change property taxes rather than some other tax? If distributional effects were unimportant, one might focus on the impact of property taxes on saving.

Unfortunately, precise answers to the first two questions are unavailable. Furthermore, as the foregoing pages have suggested, both the distributional consequences and the political significance of reduced reliance on property taxation would be great. Theoretical analysis indicates that a tax on capital tends normally to shrink the capital stock, the remuneration to labor, and total production. The first effect comes about because a tax on capital curtails saving by all except those with relatively fixed demands for consumption in the future;[52] the second because the reduction in the capital stock implies that workers have lower productivity; and the third because the other two may induce some decline in the supply of labor.[53]

Theoretical analysis gives no indication, however, whether these effects are large or small or when they will occur. The outcome depends on how sensitive saving rates are to the rate of return and on the relative saving propensities of groups that are burdened differently by the property tax and an alternative revenue source. Analysis suggests that if saving is reduced by a tax on capital, most of the burden remains with capital, but a sizable fraction can fall on labor.[54]

The actual impact of the rate of return on saving must be settled

52. The person committed to sending children to college or to achieving a given retirement nestegg must save more to reach that goal if a tax on capital reduces net yield. For a theoretical examination of the conditions under which a decline in the rate of return will raise or lower saving, see Richard A. Musgrave, *The Theory of Public Finance: A Study in Public Economy* (McGraw-Hill, 1959), p. 264; and M. S. Feldstein and S. C. Tsiang, "The Interest Rate, Taxation, and the Personal Savings Incentive," *Quarterly Journal of Economics,* vol. 82 (August 1968), pp. 419–34.

53. See Martin Feldstein, "Incidence of a Capital Income Tax in a Growing Economy with Variable Savings Rates," *Review of Economic Studies,* vol. 4 (October 1974), pp. 505–13, and Marian Krzyzaniak, "The Burden of a Differential Tax on Profits in a Neoclassical World," *Public Finance,* vol. 23, no. 4 (1968), pp. 447–77.

54. Feldstein presents numerical examples in which labor eventually bears up to one-third of a tax on capital; see "Incidence of a Capital Income Tax."

empirically. Despite the importance of the subject, relatively little evidence is available, and that is inconclusive. Some economists have detected a small positive effect of the rate of return on saving; others have detected negative effects; and some have pointed out biases in most of the attempts at measurement that render them essentially useless.[55] Other economists have noted the almost preternatural constancy of saving over many decades during which massive changes have occurred in taxes, income, and virtually every other factor alleged to affect it.[56] The failure to detect an impact of *all* tax policy on the rate of saving makes it quite difficult to assign any influence on capital accumulation to the property tax. Note that whether or not investment demand is sensitive to the rate of return is quite unimportant; if tax policy affects investment demand but not saving, it merely shifts investment from one sector to another without changing total capital accumulation.[57] Even if it should turn out that property taxes do have a sizable impact on saving, fiscal and monetary tools are available to offset it.

Whatever these effects may be, average tax rates on capital obviously changed little from the 1950s through the mid-1960s (see table 3-7). While effective rates of property taxation rose, corpora-

55. For findings of positive effects, see Colin Wright, "Saving and the Rate of Interest," in Arnold C. Harberger and Martin J. Bailey (eds.), *The Taxation of Income from Capital* (Brookings Institution, 1969), pp. 275–300; W. H. Somermeyer and R. Bannink, *A Consumption Savings Model and Its Applications* (American Elsevier, 1973), pp. 348–50. For findings of negative effects, see Warren Weber, "The Effect of Interest Rates on Aggregate Consumption," *American Economic Review*, vol. 60 (September 1970), pp. 591–600. For the biases, see Martin S. Feldstein, "Inflation, Specification Bias, and the Impact of Interest Rates," *Journal of Political Economy*, vol. 78 (November/December 1970), pp. 1325–39. The bias in previous studies derived from the use of nominal interest rates to measure yield. Feldstein argued that real interest rates—the nominal rate less the expected rate of inflation—should have been used because part of the nominal yield during periods of inflation serves only to compensate holders of fixed-value assets for the decline in the real value of their assets. Wright attempted crudely to deal with this problem in his study.

56. Edward F. Denison, "A Note on Private Saving," *Review of Economics and Statistics*, vol. 40 (August 1958), pp. 261–67; Paul A. David and John L. Scadding, "Private Savings: Ultrarationality, Aggregation, and 'Denison's Law,'" *Journal of Political Economy*, vol. 82 (March/April 1974), pp. 225–49.

57. For differing views on the sensitivity of investment demand to various tax incentives, see Gary Fromm (ed.), *Tax Incentives and Capital Spending* (Brookings Institution, 1971). For evidence on the shift effects, see Henry J. Aaron, Frank S. Russek, Jr., and Neil M. Singer, "Tax Changes and Composition of Fixed Investment: An Aggregative Simulation," *Review of Economics and Statistics*, vol. 54 (November 1972), pp. 343–56 (Brookings Reprint 257).

Table 3-7. Property Taxes and Other Capital Taxes as a Percentage of Income from Capital, Major Industries, 1953–59 and 1963–69

| | 1953–59 | | | 1963–69 | | |
Industry	Property taxes	Other	Total	Property taxes	Other	Total
Agriculture	16.5	0.9	17.4	25.1	1.2	26.3
Mining	10.9	19.4	30.3	13.2	21.5	34.7
Contract construction	9.2	27.2	36.4	11.0	20.0	31.0
Manufacturing	6.7	40.7	47.4	7.0	36.4	43.4
Transportation	17.6	28.3	45.8	21.2	14.7	35.9
Communication	13.8	39.3	53.1	10.2	37.3	47.4
Electric, gas, etc.	18.5	30.9	49.4	17.8	26.4	44.2
Trade	9.2	22.9	32.1	12.8	19.5	32.3
Services	15.9	18.1	34.0	18.9	12.4	31.3
Real estate	26.7	1.2	27.9	32.1	0.6	32.7
All industries	14.2	23.1	37.3	18.0	18.9	36.9

Sources: 1953–59—Leonard G. Rosenberg, "Taxation of Income from Capital, by Industry Group," in Arnold C. Harberger and Martin J. Bailey (eds.), *The Taxation of Income from Capital* (Brookings Institution, 1969), table 14, pp. 174–77.

1963–69—Thomas E. Vasquez, "Differential Taxation of Income from Capital in the U.S., 1963–1969: Analysis and Measurement" (Ph.D. dissertation, Clark University, no date), tables 3.7 and 3.9, pp. 47, 49. These estimates include severance taxes of $559 million, excluded by Rosenberg.

Details may not add to totals due to rounding.

tion income taxes fell, leaving the ratio of capital taxes to total capital income virtually unchanged. The industrial composition of capital taxation has shifted so as to reduce differences among major industry groups: the four industries subject to heaviest taxation during 1953–59 experienced declines in overall tax rates while the three industries subject to lightest taxation experienced rises.[58] Since the mid-1960s inflation has increased the burdensomeness of the corporation income tax because depreciation allowances are based on historical cost, not on replacement cost, and because inventory profits (the increase in the price level between purchase and sale of inventories) are subject to tax although they do not constitute a real gain to the firm.[59]

58. Recent work by Stiglitz suggests that the data in table 3-7, though relevant for comparing average tax burdens on capital in various industries, give no indication of marginal tax rates applicable to additional units of investment. Stiglitz argues that, roughly speaking, the corporation income tax on capital investments does not affect business investment decisions. One may infer from his analysis that the property tax would affect such decisions because average and marginal rates are equal. See Joseph E. Stiglitz, "Taxation, Corporate Financial Policy, and the Cost of Capital," *Journal of Public Economics*, vol. 2 (February 1973), pp. 1–34.

59. See William D. Nordhaus, "The Falling Share of Profits," *Brookings Papers on Economic Activity* (1:1974), pp. 169–208.

Table 3-7 refutes the frequent contention that real estate is subject to unreasonable tax burdens because of the property tax. Capital used in real estate plainly is taxed more heavily under the property tax than is capital used in any other industry. But it virtually escapes the corporation income tax. Furthermore, the property tax burden on housing is reduced for owner-occupants by sizable personal income tax advantages, which in 1975 held their total income tax liability more than $10.2 billion below what it would have been if their investment in their own homes were taxed like other investments.[60] Consequently, the total tax rate applicable to capital invested in real estate is less than that borne by capital in most other sectors.[61]

Market Imperfections and Incidence

All of the foregoing analysis rests on the assumption that owners of real property attempt roughly to maximize long-run profits and are free from external constraints in this search. Whether they operate in highly competitive or imperfectly competitive markets or are monopolists, whether they practice racial or economic discrimination or are color blind, the validity of the new view of property tax incidence is unaffected.[62] But there are special situations in which the traditional view is more nearly correct. One is a period marked by rent control, when excess demand exists and the authorities permit landlords to treat property tax increases as a legitimate reason for raising rents. In such a case, incidence is asymmetrical: a decrease in property taxes would benefit owners, not renters. The traditional view may also be correct in the short run if landlords set rents collusively, but not at the level that maximizes profits, and use changes in property taxes as an excuse for raising rents. How-

60. The $10.2 billion estimate is taken from *Special Analyses, Budget of the United States Government, Fiscal Year 1976*, table F-1, p. 109. This amount is the tax saving for owner-occupants due to deductibility of mortgage interest and property taxes. Owner-occupants enjoy additional tax savings from the exclusion from taxable income of net imputed rent. For an explanation of why these items should be included in taxable income, see Aaron, "Income Taxes and Housing," and Aaron, *Shelter and Subsidies*.

61. See Helen Ladd, "The Role of the Property Tax: A Reassessment," in Richard A. Musgrave (ed.), *Broad-Based Taxes: New Options and Sources* (Johns Hopkins University Press, 1973), pp. 59–64, 67–68.

62. The notion that the validity of the new view is undermined if producers engage in markup pricing was shown to be incorrect by Harberger, "Incidence of the Corporation Income Tax."

ever, such collusion is unlikely to be extensive because nearly all housing markets are highly competitive, with widely diffused ownership.[63]

Property taxes on regulated utilities pose another problem for the new view. Regulatory agencies usually set rates to allow the utility a target rate of return on capital investment, after deduction of all expenses including property taxes. Thus, an increase in taxes can justify an increase in rates, a process that appears to guarantee that users will bear the property taxes on utilities. Moreover, profits in these industries depend on the quantity of capital employed, because regulatory agencies generally base utility charges on the *rate* of return. Accordingly, in contrast with other industries in a similar situation, utilities are unlikely to respond to higher property taxes by reducing the amount of capital they use per unit of output. To the extent that the demand they face is price elastic, however, a rate increase will curtail their need for capital and reduce the price other industries must pay for it. This statement rests on the assumption that utilities are more capital intensive than the industries to which demand would shift as utility demand diminished. If the reverse were true, an increase in property taxes on utilities might raise the rate of return on capital. One cannot conclude from the rate-setting process alone, however, that property taxes on utilities are exactly borne by users.

Conclusion

Policymakers and citizens ask a variety of questions about the property tax. A local official wants to know how burdens on his constituents will change if he succeeds in getting the state to remit proceeds from an income tax increase to localities, permitting him to cut property tax rates. A national official wants to know how tax burdens in general will change if numerous states and localities adopt such a change, and also what would happen if federal taxes are remitted to localities. A citizen is curious about whether the increase in property tax rates since the 1950s has made the tax system more progressive or more regressive.

63. For an explanation of the special circumstances under which the traditional view may be correct, see Ladd, "Role of the Property Tax," pp. 46–51; Richard A. Musgrave, "Is a Property Tax on Housing Regressive?" in American Economic Association, *Papers and Proceedings of the Eighty-sixth Annual Meeting, 1973* (*American Economic Review*, vol. 64, May 1974), pp. 222–29.

Both the traditional and the new views of property tax incidence help to answer these questions. The traditional view gives the correct answer to the first question. Because the cost of capital to a single locality is determined in national markets, a local decision to change taxes will not affect it. If property taxes are cut, local users of taxed property can reduce the prices of goods they produce and still cover the nationally determined cost of capital. Hence, the tax cut will benefit consumers of goods whose price is determined in local markets, such as housing. It may also benefit landowners, laborers, or owners of capital used in producing goods whose prices are determined in national markets. Landowners would benefit directly from the tax cut and indirectly from any increase in the demand for land that might ensue.

The other three questions should be approached with the new view. The national official's questions concern a change in property taxes that is essentially national in scope (with local variations, perhaps, in its degree), so that changes in the aggregate rate of return to owners of capital must be considered. A general decrease in property taxes, brought about by substitution of the income tax or a value-added tax, would tend to increase the after-tax yield from taxed capital. Similarly, a general increase in property tax rates, such as occurred during the 1950s and 1960s, would reduce the after-tax yield. These results contrast sharply with analysis based on the traditional view, under which consumers, especially renters, appear to bear the brunt.

The correct answer to the citizen's query about the developments during the 1950s and 1960s is that they made the tax system more progressive. A general decline in property taxation would make it less so. However, residents of communities contemplating a change in rates are likely to consider only the impact on their own jurisdictions—the excise-type effects. They will perceive that raising property taxes, rather than state sales or income taxes, may depress local land values, hinder local industry, or raise the prices of local goods and services. They may not perceive, and in any case are unlikely to be influenced by, the individually small but collectively significant impact of their decision on taxpayers elsewhere. That the property tax has continued to rise in the face of such obvious disincentives can be readily explained, however, by the political niche it occupies: it is the one major tax local officials can administer and can adjust to pay for the public services they are asked to provide.

CHAPTER FOUR

Tax Capitalization and Administrative Reform

To find a value good and true,
Here are three things for you to do:
Consider your replacement cost,
Determine value that is lost,
Analyze your sales to see
What market value really should be.
Now if these suggestions are not clear,
Copy the figures you used last year.
Anonymous[1]

FOR MOST MORTALS, mere mention of property tax administration is sufficient to make eyes glaze over and heads nod. Except when tax bills arrive and are compared with the neighbor's, the odor of dusty ledgers and the aura of green eyeshades kill the attention of all but the interested few. For economists, especially, the subject of

1. Quoted, in describing the role of assessors, in *Property Taxation: Effects on Land Uses and Local Government Revenues*, A study prepared for the Subcommittee on Intergovernmental Relations of the Senate Committee on Government Operations, 92 Cong. 1 sess. (1971), p. 29.

tax administration has carried none of the allure of "analysis" or "policy," but only the drabness of bureaucratic affairs.

This inattention is unfortunate because proposed reforms in the administration of the property tax are central to issues of public policy and have considerable analytic interest. These issues closely resemble those raised by social reformers and economists who have argued that property taxes should be replaced by a land-value tax, a value-added tax, or some other source of revenue. In each case, the problem is that large changes in the perceived net worth of many households would follow sizable changes in property tax rates. This chapter will describe these issues. It will indicate that the case for reform is not so simple and straightforward as its proponents have argued and that, in some cases, "inequitable" administration may be defensible.[2]

What Is "Equal" Administration?

In most taxing jurisdictions, the law requires all properties to be taxed at the same effective rate. This common rate results from the application of a single nominal rate to assessed values, all of which are to be the same proportion of market value. Some states permit localities to assess special classes of property at different proportions of market value, and some permit or require different nominal rates for various classes of property. Within each class, however, the same rate is supposed to apply. If legal standards were fully met, one would observe a clustering of effective rates around the average in each tax-rate area.[3] In fact, the large coefficients of dispersion cited in chapter 2 show that the legal standards are not met. Each jurisdiction contains a wide range of effective rates.

Capitalization of Differentials in Property Tax Rates

That variation in effective tax rates within taxing jurisdictions is contrary to law is unquestionable. The economic consequences are

2. For an independent and general application of the type of analysis used in this chapter, see Martin Feldstein, "On the Theory of Tax Reform" (paper presented for the Conference on Taxation of the International Seminar in Public Economics, Paris, January 1975; processed).

3. Since taxing jurisdictions overlap, equal composite rates would prevail only in neighborhoods covered by the same jurisdictions.

far harder to unravel. Assume that all properties within each jurisdiction were subject to the same effective rate of taxation. If all
property owners consumed local public services that cost exactly
as much as the property taxes they paid, both on the average and
at the margin, these taxes would serve precisely as a price of local
public services, and variations in taxes and in public services across
communities would be correlated. Given free mobility of households
and democratic local decisionmaking, variations in property tax
rates across communities would then have no effect on property
values. This process requires a very large number of communities
with diverse levels of public services and housing stocks.[4] Within
jurisdictions, property tax rates also would serve as prices if their
variations matched those in the consumption of local public services.

Unfortunately, not only is there no reason to believe in such a
neat congruence between variations in tax collections and in local
public services, either across communities or within them, but in
fact the two vary quite independently of one another. If such variations are persistent, particularly among adjoining jurisdictions, they
are likely to be reflected in property values—that is, to be capitalized. Capitalization occurs when the price of the property bearing
the unusual tax falls below (or rises above) that of otherwise equally
valuable properties just enough to make the total cost of owning
them the same. In that event, variations in property tax rates cease
to affect locational choice. To put the matter the other way, these
variations affect locational choice only if they have not been fully
capitalized into property values.

Variations in property tax rates within jurisdictions likewise may
be capitalized into property values, most likely when they are expected to persist. If such capitalization has been crystallized in a
market sale, the present owner, in reality, will not benefit from a
below-average tax rate or suffer from an excessive rate.[5]

---

4. The text discussion is based on Bruce Hamilton, "The Effects of Property
Taxes and Local Public Spending on Property Values: A Theoretical Comment,"
Journal of Political Economy (forthcoming). See also, Bruce Hamilton, Craig Mac-
Farlane, and Peter Mieszkowski, "The Efficiency and Distributive Aspects of
Zoning" (undated manuscript).

5. Let the annual rental value of a particular property be R, the prevailing discount rate r, the average tax rate t, and the tax rate on the particular property t'.
If property taxes are fully capitalized, the value of a property assessed such that
its rate is t' is $R/(r + t')$ and the capitalized value of the tax differential as a

Sources of Unequal Administration

Some tax differentials arise because assessors intentionally apply different standards to different properties, others because the valuation of property is not an exact science; but they share one characteristic—they are illegal. Should the law be changed, and, if so, how?

Intentional Inequalities

Intentional inequalities arise when tax administrators purposely reduce assessments for certain taxpayers. They do so out of a variety of motives. They may wish to induce certain firms to locate or to remain within the jurisdiction because the firms will pay more taxes than the value of public services they will consume or because they will provide jobs and thereby increase local income and property values. The authorities may wish to induce middle- and upper-class residents to remain within the jurisdiction or to discourage poor or black families from entering. They may seek to propitiate owners of single-family homes, whose voting power and sensitivity to property taxes are legend. In some cases, commercial and, especially, industrial interests manage to secure lower property taxes than can other owners.

In 1971, among the twenty-five largest cities in the United States, single-family properties were taxed more lightly than multifamily dwellings in eighteen and more lightly than commercial and industrial properties in sixteen (see table 4-1). In six cities (New York, Chicago, Cleveland, Milwaukee, San Diego, and Boston) the underassessment of single-family housing relative to commercial and industrial property was so great that no explanation other than intentional discrimination seems adequate. In two cities (Memphis and St. Louis) the reverse pattern is apparent. The underassessment of single-family housing relative to multifamily housing seems too large to be explained by random error in nine cities (New York, Philadelphia, Baltimore, Dallas, Indianapolis, Boston, St. Louis, Phoenix, and Seattle).

---

fraction of the undistorted market value is $[(r + t)/(r + t')] - 1$. When t' exceeds t, properties subject to tax at the rate t' sell at a discount; when t exceeds t', properties sell at a premium.

Table 4-1. Relative Assessment Rates on Selected Classes of Property in the Twenty-five Largest U.S. Cities, 1971

Percent of average assessment rates for all properties; city-wide average = 100

	Housing		Commercial-industrial
City	Single-family	Multifamily	
New York	71	108	151
Chicago	95	111	145
Los Angeles	104	93	109
Philadelphia	94	114	110
Detroit	99	109	108
Houston	102	119	98
Baltimore	97	140	103
Dallas	89	136	100
Washington, D.C.	98	112	92
Cleveland	97	106	128
Indianapolis	100	139	90
Milwaukee	99	104	121
San Francisco	106	91	108
San Diego	82	75	181
San Antonio	101	88	102
Boston	75	101	167
Honolulu	101	92	95
Memphis	100	109	67
St. Louis	105	135	76
New Orleans	101	101	110
Phoenix	93	117	104
Columbus	104	82	88
Seattle	94	140	n.a.
Pittsburgh	99	105	86
Denver	97	108	103

Source: Calculated from U.S. Bureau of the Census, 1972 Census of Governments, unpublished tabulations.

n.a. Not available.

Property tax administration in Boston illustrates these characteristics in classic form, and in addition exhibits sharp discrimination between new and old nonresidential property. The effective rate of tax on new commercial property is 3.7 percent of market value, compared with 10.6 percent on old commercial property; the average rate on all commercial property is 8.2 percent compared with 5.5 percent on residential property.[6] Within the category of resi-

6. Daniel M. Holland and Oliver Oldman, "Estimating the Impact of 100% of Market Value Property Tax Assessments of Boston Real Estate" (Boston Urban Observatory, August 1974; processed), table 3, p. 8.

dential property the assessment-sales ratio on single-family houses is only 60 percent of that on apartment houses with six or more dwellings.[7] But this practice is by no means unique to Boston.

An argument can be made in principle for some variations in effective tax rates, on the grounds that they can benefit localities and the nation. The case rests on matching—as closely as is feasible— local taxes for each property to its consumption of local public services, on the theory that, otherwise, economic activities are mis-allocated and income is redistributed by localities, a level of government not well equipped for this task.[8] In the case of large properties, localities can sometimes evaluate approximately the local public services consumed and determine the adequacy of tax payments. When payments of particular owners exceed the cost of the local public services they consume and any external costs they impose on other owners, it is consistent with efficient allocation to reduce their taxes accordingly. Conversely, owners who consume public services costing more than the taxes they generate should be subject to heavier taxes.

Even stronger arguments can be made against such variations in tax rates—apart from the absence of hard evidence that actual negotiations between taxpayers and assessors achieve the optimal pattern. Even if it were possible accurately to measure the consumption of local public services, the process by which tax reductions are negotiated is ill suited to balancing tax payments and these costs. Typically, special agreements are negotiated informally and secretly between tax assessors and property owners who may negotiate separately with a large number of communities and play one off against another. Tax assessors, untrained and unrehearsed in the role, are cast as judges of the total value to a community of a particular business or residential complex. If the firm is an important local em-

7. "Averages of Ratios of Assessed Value to Sales Price for Property Sold in City of Boston, January 1, 1960, through October 10, 1968" (unpublished tabulations by Henry Aaron and Oliver Oldman). The 60 percent figure in the text is for 1968. For published data covering earlier years, see Oliver Oldman and Henry Aaron, "Assessment–Sales Ratios under the Boston Property Tax," *National Tax Journal*, vol. 18 (March 1965), pp. 36–49; reprinted in *Assessors Journal*, vol. 4 (April 1969), pp. 13–29.

8. For an argument that local governments are ill equipped to redistribute income, see Richard A. Musgrave and Peggy B. Musgrave, *Public Finance in Theory and Practice* (McGraw-Hill, 1973), p. 606. For a contrasting view, see Mark V. Pauly, "Income Redistribution as a Local Public Good," *Journal of Public Economics*, vol. 2 (February 1973), pp. 35–58.

ployer, it can threaten to depart and to disrupt the local economy. In such circumstances, the prospect that negotiations will equate tax bills and the value of local services consumed is slight. Such negotiations enable these property owners to extort hidden subsidies. They are natural forums for bribery. And they are illegal. Even if they were carried out in the open, subject to legal standards and safeguards, they would be subject to the criticism that tax incentives affecting many communities should be determined at the regional or national level, not by local governments individually pursuing their perceived self-interest.[9]

Tax concessions to middle- or upper-income households to encourage their continued residence in a jurisdiction, or to homeowners in general to reduce discontent with incumbent officials, are subject to many of the same objections and others as well. Since middle- and upper-income neighborhoods have considerable continuity, tax concessions to them are likely to be perceived as permanent, and capitalized into property values. Eventually, therefore, middle- and upper-income homeowners will find that the price of houses within the concession-granting jurisdiction is higher relative to surrounding communities than otherwise would have been the case. At this point nothing discourages the current owners from cashing in the increase in value by selling and moving. Even more important, since the tax concession has been capitalized into a market price, it no longer constitutes an incentive to prospective buyers to locate within that jurisdiction. In short, favorable tax treatment for middle- and upper-income households amounts to a capital grant to such households and a capital levy on lower-income homeowners and other property owners whose property values are reduced by taxes that are higher than would be necessary if rates were equal. Moreover, the tax concession influences the residential choice of neither the rich nor the poor once it has been capitalized.[10]

9. Grieson raises the intriguing possibility that assessors might use discrimination in administration to minimize the "deadweight loss" from property taxes—to keep at a minimum the distortions in economic decisions caused by the property taxes. He offers no evidence, however, that they in fact behave in this manner. Ronald E. Grieson, "The Economics of Property Taxes and Land Values: The Elasticity of Supply of Structures," *Journal of Urban Economics*, vol. 1 (October 1974), pp. 377–80.

10. If homeowners do not understand the forces that have caused prices to rise (if they attribute the gains to, say, "neighborhood quality," rather than to tax

Unintentional Inequalities

Not all variations in assessment-sales ratios among classes of property result from active discrimination. Unintentional inequalities arise because the determination of market values of real property is not an exact science, because the administration of the property tax is costly, and because many administrators do not use available resources efficiently to estimate market values. In general, the degree of unintended inequalities depends on the variation in rates of growth of property values, the period between reassessments, and the accuracy of each assessment.[11] As a result of the influences, the dispersion of assessment-sales ratios tends to rise (possibly reaching a limit) if reassessments are not carried out. Increases in the dispersion of assessment-sales ratios are the consequence of a failure to reassess.[12] Thus, coefficients of dispersion (or other measures of variation) measure the inequity in the distribution of tax shares relative to the legal standard.

The amount each taxing jurisdiction spends on tax administration expresses the importance it attaches to an equitable sharing of tax burdens. Assume some valid measure of the inequality of tax administration, I (for example, the coefficient of variation); that the costs of reducing I increase as I declines; and that the offensiveness of unequal assessments rises as I increases.[13] Then expenditures on tax administration should be set at the point where the expenditures for improving administration (through more frequent or more accurate assessment) just equals the utility of the decrease in inequity that they buy. In effect, the budget for tax administration expresses the value placed on distributing tax burdens according to law.[14]

---

concessions), and if they have elastic price expectations, the relative growth in property values resulting from tax concessions may lead them to anticipate further growth and to retain ownership because the quality of their homes as investment goods, not as consumer goods, seems to have been enhanced.

11. For an empirical investigation of the importance of these factors, see Morton Paglin and Michael Fogarty, "Equity and the Property Tax: A New Conceptual Focus," *National Tax Journal*, vol. 25 (December 1972), pp. 557–65.

12. Robert F. Engle, "De Facto Discrimination in Residential Assessments: Boston" (rev., Massachusetts Institute of Technology, December 1974; processed).

13. These two assumptions can be expressed, respectively, as follows: $dI/dC < 0$ and $d^2I/dC^2 > 0$, where C is cost; and for some loss function, $L(I)$, $dL/dI > 0$.

14. The formal relationships underlying the statements in this paragraph are set forth in app. B.

No clear line can be drawn between intentional and unintentional inequalities. For example, if the market values of identifiable groups of properties are changing systematically at different rates, a decision to reassess less frequently has the effect of increasing both the relative overassessment of properties whose value is rising less than average and the relative underassessment of properties appreciating more rapidly than average.[15] When elected officials decide how much to spend on administration, they decide how much inequality they will permit (assuming that assessors are instructed to be fair and impartial). Where unintentional inequalities persist and are recognized by sellers and buyers, they will be capitalized in the same fashion as are intentional inequalities. The key to capitalization is the existence of persistent tax differentials, whatever the motive for their creation. Permitting the continuance of unintentional inequalities in tax burdens that are not capitalized can be justified only if the cost of removing them is considered excessive.

The Case against Property Tax Reform

When property tax differentials are created and capitalized, they generate one-time capital gains or losses in property values. If current owners acquired the property *before* such capitalization, removal of a tax differential merely cancels unrealized capital gains or losses. If current owners acquired the property *after* capitalization, removal of a tax differential will do nothing to recapture the capital gains enjoyed, or to repay the capital losses suffered, by previous owners. It will, however, inflict capital losses (if the rate had been too low) or bestow capital gains (if the rate had been too high) on current owners, because, as far as their real costs are concerned, a tax differential does not exist. In short, tax reform creates rather than removes inequities if tax differentials have been capitalized and the property sold.

Removing tax differentials, whether within or among jurisdictions, will have the same effects (if local public services are unaffected). In considering the pitfalls for general property tax relief, the Advisory Commission on Intergovernmental Relations correctly observes that

a sudden change in property taxes will affect how investors view the market and could result in some dramatic economic effects. . . .

Because the property tax is deeply entrenched in the capital structure,

15. See ibid., and chap. 3, note 25.

the economic consequences of a drastic reduction, say 50 percent for all classes of property, should be taken into account when property tax relief is proposed. Owners of land, whether occupied or vacant, would reap large gains. Owners of houses and other buildings would experience somewhat smaller gains.[16]

Yet these effects seldom give concern to those who advocate equal administration. Differences in property tax rates across jurisdictional boundaries are seen as matters of tax policy, worthy of debate and political resolution; those within boundaries are seen as mere matters of administration, a boring subject for boring people.[17]

The asymmetrical approach to tax differentials across and within jurisdictional boundaries has some, but only some, justification. Tax differentials between jurisdictions may persist because of differences in tastes for public services or because one jurisdiction has large businesses or utilities that generate revenue more than sufficient to pay for the local public services they consume. Some tax differentials within jurisdictions are transitory, ebbing and flowing with the assessment cycle; but many persist because they are due to basic flaws in tax administration or to quasi-legal or illegal decisions by the taxing authorities to favor particular groups.

The practical question concerns the degree to which variations in property tax rates within or across jurisdictions are capitalized into property values. Evidence on this subject is sparse, because it is difficult to obtain data that permit clean measurement of capitalization; but a growing number of studies indicates that property tax differentials, both across and within jurisdictions, are fully capitalized.[18]

16. Advisory Commission on Intergovernmental Relations, *Financing Schools and Property Tax Relief—A State Responsibility* (ACIR, 1973), pp. 83, 85.

17. One author recently paraphrased Lord Acton: "Government tends to be boring and local government bores absolutely," and queried whether local government officials are "so dedicated they don't mind being bored? So boring they appear dedicated?" Calvin Trillin, "U.S. Journal: Houston—Some Thoughts at a Congress of Cities," *New Yorker* (January 6, 1975), p. 57.

18. For analysis of cross-jurisdiction differentials, see Wallace E. Oates, "The Effects of Property Taxes and Local Public Spending on Property Values: An Empirical Study of Tax Capitalization and the Tiebout Hypothesis," *Journal of Political Economy*, vol. 77 (November/December 1969), pp. 957–71. Also see F. O. Woodard and Ronald W. Brady, "Inductive Evidence of Tax Capitalization," *National Tax Journal*, vol. 18 (June 1965), pp. 193–201; Larry L. Orr, "The Incidence of Differential Property Taxes on Urban Housing," *National Tax Journal*, vol. 21 (September 1968), pp. 253–62. For critical comments on Orr, see Robert M. Coen and Brian J. Powell, "Theory and Measurement of the Incidence

The Case for Reform

Even if all property tax differentials were fully capitalized, a case could be made for their removal within jurisdictions. First, the capitalized value of many tax differentials has not been realized through sales, and their removal will prevent the realization of at least some accrued gains or losses that were created, not by changes in the real services a property provides its owner, but by the assessor. Second, differences in tax rates affect the price of maintenance and improvements on existing structures. Owners who undertake improvements or maintenance will enjoy below-average net rates of return on these expenditures if they bear above-average taxes, and vice versa, other things held constant. Thus, some improvements with above-average returns may be forgone while others with below-average returns are undertaken as a result of tax differentials. For this reason, tax differentials are a source of inefficiency.

The fear that improvements may trigger reassessment and upward revaluation and the belief that such fears inhibit improvements are both widespread. Note that it is the *anticipated marginal* tax occasioned by the change in value due to maintenance expenditures or capital improvements, not the *actual* marginal tax or the *average* tax, that is relevant. Some evidence suggests that on deteriorating or slum properties many improvements are ignored, perhaps because assessors recognize that tax rates on such properties are already above average.[19] Third, new inequities are created with every unanticipated change in tax rates or property values.

---

of Differential Property Taxes on Rental Housing," and John D. Heinberg and Wallace E. Oates, "The Incidence of Differential Property Taxes on Rental Housing: An Addendum," both in *National Tax Journal*, vol. 25 (June 1972), pp. 211–16 and 221–22, respectively.

For analysis of within-jurisdiction differentials, see Albert M. Church, "Capitalization of the Effective Property Tax Rate on Single Family Residences," *National Tax Journal*, vol. 27 (March 1974), pp. 113–22; John H. Wicks, Robert A. Little, and Ralph A. Beck, "A Note on Capitalization of Property Tax Changes," *National Tax Journal*, vol. 21 (September 1968), pp. 263–65; R. Stafford Smith, "Property Tax Capitalization in San Francisco," *National Tax Journal*, vol. 23 (June 1970), pp. 177–91. For contrary results based on data from Vancouver, British Columbia, see T. J. Wales and E. G. Wiens, "Capitalization of Residential Property Taxes: An Empirical Study," *Review of Economics and Statistics*, vol. 56 (August 1974), pp. 329–33.

19. See *A Study of Property Taxes and Urban Blight*. Prepared for the U.S. Department of Housing and Urban Development by Arthur D. Little, Inc.; printed

In short, the case against reform rests on the inequities that arise when tax differentials, already capitalized through actual sales, are removed. This process reimposes inequities with which the market has already come to terms. The case for reform rests on removing inequities not yet capitalized through actual sales, encouraging efficient maintenance and rehabilitation, and forestalling new inequities. These gains must be sufficient to overcome the inequities change would bring.

The persuasiveness of the case for reform is likely to vary according to place and time. In general, it varies with the effective tax rate; the rate of new construction, and the amount of maintenance and rehabilitation, relative to the existing tax base; the breadth of recent changes in property tax rates or values; and the proportion of administrative inequities that is due to purely transitory factors (such as the assessment cycle). In general, these considerations suggest that good administration is worth less in communities that are neither highly developed nor developing than it is in developed or expanding jurisdictions.

One of the paradoxes of property tax administration is that frequent sales make equal administration easier (because accurate benchmarks are readily available), but reduce its desirability (because persistent tax differentials are more likely to have been capitalized through actual sales). The foregoing analysis also suggests that where capitalization demonstrably has occurred, property owners whose previously favorable assessments are increased have a claim to compensation from the taxing authority. Conversely, the taxing authority could legitimately impose a lump-sum levy on owners of properties on which unfavorable taxes have been capitalized, and whose assessments are reduced. Such compensation can be defended only if tax advantages plainly have been capitalized.

Administrative Reform

Property tax administration has improved markedly over the past two decades, measured either by the technical standards of the

for the use of the Subcommittee on Intergovernmental Relations of the Senate Committee on Government Operations, 93 Cong. 1 sess. (1973), p. 10, and table B, p. 12. Although no property improvements led to reassessment in blighted areas that were surveyed, many owners cited fear of reassessment as a reason for not undertaking improvements (ibid., p. 11).

Bureau of the Census or by the professionalism of procedures and personnel in property tax jurisdictions.[20] Coefficients of dispersion declined (at least until 1966) at the same time that—and perhaps because—assessing districts grew through consolidation, the training and schooling of administrative personnel improved, more independent appeal and review boards were established, and ratio studies and disclosure of their results spread. Much additional improvement is needed, however. Among forty-nine states and the District of Columbia that replied to a survey carried out by the Senate Subcommittee on Intergovernmental Relations, only twelve reported that all local assessors are appointed; the other thirty-eight require some or all assessors to face elections, thereby tempting them to court political favor with discriminatory assessments. Only thirty-three of the states carry out studies of assessment-sales ratios.[21]

The property tax remains one of the most unpopular taxes in the United States, so disliked that it became a major issue in the 1972 presidential campaign.[22] Part of its unpopularity, no doubt, flows from the increases in property tax bills over the past two decades. But the capitalization of past tax differentials suggests that the process of improving administration may make the property tax even more unpopular, at least temporarily. The removal of tax differentials, built into the price at which past sales were executed, generates windfall gains and losses for current owners.

While regular reassessment, on a three- to eight-year cycle,[23] is

20. On the latter, see Ronald B. Welch, "The Way We Were—Four Decades of Change in the Property Tax" (paper prepared for delivery at the 1974 annual meeting of the National Association of Tax Administrators; processed).

21. *Status of Property Tax Administration in the States*, Prepared by the Subcommittee on Intergovernmental Relations of the Senate Committee on Government Operations, 93 Cong. 1 sess. (1973), p. 11. See also U.S. Bureau of the Census, *Property Assessment Ratio Studies*, State and Local Government Special Studies no. 52 (no date).

22. A poll taken in March 1972 by the Advisory Commission on Intergovernmental Relations asked respondents which tax they felt was "the worst tax—that is, the least fair." Forty-five percent named the property tax. The federal income tax was a distant second at 19 percent, with state income and sales taxes tied at 13 percent; 11 percent "didn't know." By April 1974, removed from the glare of a presidential campaign, the property tax was named by only 28 percent of all respondents, slightly behind the federal income tax (30 percent), but still ahead of state sales taxes (20 percent) and state income taxes (10 percent). Advisory Commission on Intergovernmental Relations, "Changing Public Attitudes on Governments and Taxes" (ACIR, 1974; processed), table 3.

23. See Paglin and Fogarty, "Equity and the Property Tax," p. 560.

becoming increasingly common, the jump in taxes at reassessment may be 50 percent or more, especially in rapidly appreciating areas.[24] When such increases are combined with a correction in long-standing underassessment, the shock to taxpayers can only deepen the unpopularity of the property tax.

Several administrative reforms can remove the focus for opposition to the property tax—large, discrete increases—and enhance their legitimacy. The first is a combination of full disclosure of assessment practices and norms and of a simple, cheap, speedy, and independent procedure for appeals.[25] The policy of full disclosure requires that all taxpayers be informed on their tax bills of (a) the assessed value of their property and, when fractional assessment is used, the estimated market value; (b) the average ratio of assessed values to market prices in the jurisdiction, based on studies of assessment-sales price ratios; and (c) the appeal procedures. The second reform is frequent reassessment and billing. Before the development of the high-speed computer, the cost of on-site appraisal precluded frequent reassessment. Using statistical analysis, however, administrators can now estimate changes in property values without leaving their offices, based on association between trends in market prices and such characteristics of properties as location, type, previous value, and nearby municipal improvements and private construction.[26] The state of California pioneered in the use of computer-based reassessment, and jurisdictions in other regions are now following suit. Once such systems are in operation, and the flow of information is assured, little more than clerical adjustments are required to reassess all properties annually or semiannually, thereby

---

24. See chap. 1, pp. 3–4.

25. Both have long been advocated by the Advisory Commission on Intergovernmental Relations. See, for example, *Financing Schools and Property Tax Relief—A State Responsibility*, p. 69.

26. See Henry Aaron, "Some Observations on Property Tax Valuation and the Significance of Full Value Assessment," in Arthur D. Lynn, Jr. (ed.), *The Property Tax and Its Administration* (University of Wisconsin Press, 1969), pp. 153–66; Jack Lessinger, "Econometrics and Appraisal," *Appraisal Journal*, vol. 37 (October 1969), pp. 501–12; Andrew J. Hinshaw, "The Assessor and Computerization of Data," *Appraisal Journal*, vol. 37 (April 1969), pp. 283–88; Theodore R. Smith, "Multiple Regression and the Appraisal of Single Family Residential Properties," *Appraisal Journal*, vol. 39 (April 1971), pp. 277–84; Jerome Dasso, *Computerized Assessment Administration* (Chicago: International Association of Assessing Officers, 1973); and John B. Rackham and Theodore Reynolds Smith, *Automated Mass Appraisal of Real Property* (IAAO, 1974).

reducing the size of periodic tax adjustments. Tax bills could easily be tendered quarterly or monthly instead of annually or semiannually, as they now are. Indeed, many taxpayers already make monthly tax payments along with their mortgage payments. Moreover, tax increases could be interpolated between adjustment points. In the same manner, correction of past errors could be made more palatable if introduced gradually. In combination, these changes in administration would create a system in which the taxpayer would never confront large increments in his tax bill, except in special cases such as rezoning or the discovery through on-site appraisal of errors in automatic adjustments; and all increases would enjoy legitimacy because they could be appealed. This system would contrast markedly with present arrangements, under which taxpayers are periodically told of very large increases without any explanation, and with no way to get one.

CHAPTER FIVE

Reforming the Property Tax

POPULAR DISCONTENT with the distribution of property tax liabilities has led to a wide variety of special exemptions and rebates and to suggestions that the tax base be altered. In the mistaken belief that the property tax is regressive, cash payments to low- and moderate-income homeowners and renters have been enacted in many states and are contemplated by others and by the federal government. Responding to decisions of state courts that present methods of financing elementary and secondary education violate state constitutions, some state legislatures have begun to consider ways to reduce reliance on local property taxes. Finally, a long line of economists and social reformers have urged the exemption of structures and other improvements, thus converting the property tax into a land tax that, they argue, would result in more efficient design of cities and in better land use. Although no major jurisdiction in the United States other than the city of Pittsburgh and the state of Hawaii has moved in this direction, land taxation remains a favorite among economists. This chapter will review the issues surrounding these three arguments for reform.

Tax Relief

Most states provide homestead exemptions, exemptions for senior citizens, or "circuit breaker" relief against property tax liabilities.

Homestead exemptions provide for the reduction of assessed values by some fixed amount. They exempt relatively inexpensive housing from taxation, lower effective average tax rates for owner-occupants in somewhat more expensive housing, and increase effective tax rates for all other property owners. Exemptions for senior citizens are homestead exemptions limited to the aged. These two types of tax relief are available in thirty-four states.[1] Both have been losing favor to "circuit breakers," first adopted in Wisconsin in 1964. By the end of 1974, twenty-three states had enacted circuit-breaker laws of one kind or another and others were considering them.[2] All but three have been enacted since 1970. Rarely has an idea so rapidly gained such widespread acceptance despite the weakness of the major premises on which it rests.

What Is a Circuit Breaker?

Circuit breakers provide payments to taxpayers, usually as an income tax refund equal to the excess of residential property tax liabilities over a specified fraction of income. Where renters are eligible, their property tax liabilities are presumed to equal some fraction of rent. The plans now in effect contain diverse income limits and definitions, benefit formulas, and benefit ceilings. Some limit benefits to aged homeowners; others cover all renters and homeowners; many lie in between. Only a few deny benefits to households with large net worth. Because legal provisions, incomes, and housing prices all differ, the per capita cost of existing circuit breakers ranges from less than $1 to $31.78 in the jurisdictions that use them.[3]

In fact, circuit breakers differ so radically from one another in structure and size that applying a single label to them all seriously distorts reality. Table 5-1 illustrates the diversity by showing the benefits that would accrue to fourteen hypothetical families under eight existing state plans. Plans such as those in Michigan and Vermont clearly have objectives beyond assisting the very poor or the

1. For state-by-state details of these exemptions, see Advisory Commission on Intergovernmental Relations, *Federal-State-Local Finances: Significant Features of Fiscal Federalism, 1973–74 Edition* (ACIR, 1974), table 107, pp. 179–86.

2. For a discussion of circuit breakers and details on various plans, see Advisory Commission on Intergovernmental Relations, *Property Tax Circuit-Breakers: Current Status and Policy Issues* (ACIR, 1975).

3. Ibid., p. 169.

Table 5-1. Benefits for Hypothetical Nonaged Four-Person Families and Aged Couples under Selected Circuit-Breaker Plans, Eight States, 1974

Age, family income, and tenure	Amount of property taxes or rent	State							
		Michigan	New Mexico	Oregon	Pennsyl-vania	Vermont	Colorado	West Virginia	Wisconsin
Nonaged									
$15,000									
Owner	$1,000	$285.00	$0	$0	$0	$175.00	$0	$0	$0
Owner	500	0	0	0	0	0	0	0	0
Renter	3,600a	52.20	0	0	0	0	0	0	0
$7,500									
Owner	500	142.50	0	200	0	162.50	0	0	0
Owner	300	22.50	0	200	0	0	0	0	0
Renter	2,500a	97.50	0	100	0	162.50	0	0	0
Aged									
$10,000									
Owner	1,250	500.00	0	100	0	500.00	0	0	0
Renter	3,000a	310.00	0	50	0	100.00	0	0	0
$7,500									
Owner	500	387.50	0	200	0	162.50	0	0	0
Owner	300	187.50	0	200	0	0	0	0	0
Renter	2,400a	295.50	0	100	0	142.50	0	0	0
$4,000									
Owner	500	490.00	34	360	200	320.00	300	16.50	342.80
Owner	300	290.00	34	300	200	120.00	300	16.50	182.80
Renter	1,200a	194.00	34	180	168	60.00	240	16.50	182.80

Source: Derived from data provided by Commerce Clearing House, Inc.
a. Amount shown is rent paid. The part counted as property tax varies from state to state.

aged, and provide benefits to households with incomes exceeding the U.S. median. By imposing low income limits for eligibility, some states target benefits on families with meager incomes; but in all states benefits rise with home values and rents, at least until they hit certain ceilings.

Objectives of Circuit Breakers

The diversity of circuit-breaker plans reflects the diversity of their objectives. First and most prominent is the belief, resting on faith rather than knowledge of tax incidence, that the residential property tax is regressive. Thus, the Advisory Commission on Intergovernmental Relations, the leader in popularizing circuit breakers, concluded that "regardless of the assumptions made concerning the incidence of the general property tax, it is a regressive tax for the majority of American families."[4] In the best description and defense of circuit breakers, Bendick writes that, "by offering relief only to low income persons, the program appears to reduce the overall regressiveness of the property tax."[5]

Second, regardless of whether the property tax is regressive on balance, circuit breakers are alleged to protect low-income taxpayers with unusually large liabilities or with temporarily depressed incomes. Third, circuit breakers are sometimes supported because they enable aged taxpayers to remain in homes that they might otherwise have to vacate. Such households, it is argued, frequently have paid off all mortgages and experience no out-of-pocket housing costs other than maintenance and property taxes. By rebating taxes, circuit breakers enable some of these households, whose incomes typically decline at retirement, to retain ownership and others to spend more on maintenance. In a similar vein, circuit breakers can spare households with temporarily depressed incomes the burden of meeting current tax payments.

Fourth, circuit breakers can operate as an indirect form of revenue sharing if resulting tax losses are financed by the state, since they enable localities in which low-income residents are particularly numerous to shift part of the cost of property taxes to non-

4. See Advisory Commission on Intergovernmental Relations, *Financing Schools and Property Tax Relief—A State Responsibility* (ACIR, 1973), p. 42.

5. Marc Bendick, Jr., "Designing Circuit Breaker Property Tax Relief," *National Tax Journal*, vol. 27 (March 1974), p. 21.

residents and thus to set property tax rates higher than would otherwise be acceptable. Fifth, since benefits under circuit breakers accrue largely to low-income households, they can be supported by advocates of greater income redistribution as an interim device until such large-scale programs as welfare reform or a housing allowance can be enacted.

Evaluation of Circuit Breakers

Not all circuit breakers serve these objectives equally well because, despite certain common structural features, the programs differ so widely. Moreover, some of the objectives just listed rest on plain misconceptions, while others would be served best by programs with features no circuit breaker possesses.

Tax relief in this form amounts, in fact, to an income maintenance system whose benefits are related to income and property tax payments. Circuit breakers offer a kind of housing allowance, based on a peculiar formula and providing quite modest benefits: The "allowance" pays a certain percentage of rent (imputed rent, for homeowners), once rent exceeds a certain fraction of income. For example, the Vermont circuit breaker (with Michigan's, the most generous in the country) is equivalent to a housing allowance that pays 2.5 percent of the value of a house worth more than a stipulated multiple of income—1.6 times income for families with incomes below $4,000 to 2.4 times income for families with incomes of $16,000 per year.[6] For renters the Vermont plan amounts to a housing allowance equal to a certain fraction of rent when rent exceeds a stipulated fraction of income—ranging from 20 percent for households with incomes below $4,000 per year to

6. The Vermont plan rebates property taxes in excess of given percentages of incomes, as follows:

Income class	Percent of income
Below $4,000	4.0
$ 4,000– 7,999	4.5
8,000–11,999	5.0
12,000–15,999	5.5
16,000 and above	6.0

Maximum relief is $500; 20 percent of rent is regarded as property taxes.

The text statement is based on the average effective tax rate in Vermont on FHA-insured "middle income" homes of 2.5 percent. See Advisory Commission on Intergovernmental Relations, *State-Local Finances: Significant Features and Suggested Legislation, 1972 Edition* (ACIR, 1972), p. 234.

30 percent for households with incomes of $16,000 per year. Housing allowances of this "percent-of-rent" type have been criticized because they tend to inflate rents and encourage landlords and tenants to collude in overstating them;[7] circuit breakers for renters are subject to the same criticism.

Because property tax payments are related positively to ownership of real property, a major part of net worth for most households, circuit-breaker relief is related negatively to household income and positively to net worth. Thus, families whose incomes are temporarily depressed and whose housing expenditures are based on their normally higher incomes will qualify for more relief than will households whose incomes are normally low and who base their housing expenditures on those levels. Circuit breakers based on annual rather than normal income and lacking limits on net worth provide the largest benefits within each income bracket to families with the greatest net worth.[8] They tend to subsidize (a) those within each income bracket who consume unusually large amounts of housing or who have unusually large ratios of property to current income and (b) those with fluctuating incomes. The customary justifications for income redistribution do not seem to apply to these groups. Gaffney has put the point acidly: "Those that become welfare cases should be treated by the welfare system on an impartial basis, without special favor to property owners. To use property tax relief as a substitute for welfare is to distribute welfare in proportion to wealth, surely an odd notion."[9]

The efficiency of circuit breakers in meeting the stated objectives may now be evaluated directly. First, the contention that the residential property tax is regressive, though deeply ingrained, is

7. See Ira S. Lowry, "Housing Assistance for Low-Income Urban Families: A Fresh Approach," in *Papers Submitted to Subcommittee on Housing Panels on Housing Production, Housing Demand, and Developing a Suitable Living Environment*, House Committee on Banking and Currency, 92 Cong. 1 sess. (1971), pp. 489–523.

8. For calculations based on the formula contained in S. 1255, the Muskie-Percy bill to provide federal support for state circuit breakers, and supporting this contention, see Henry J. Aaron, "What Do Circuit-Breaker Laws Accomplish?" in George E. Peterson (ed.), *Property Tax Reform* (Urban Institute, 1973), pp. 53–64.

9. Mason Gaffney, "The Property Tax and Intergovernmental Relations" (remarks to the President's Advisory Commission on Intergovernmental Relations, September 14, 1972; processed), p. 4.

generally unsupported by contemporary analysis. Circuit-breaker relief for renters may be justified under the traditional view that the residential property tax is regressive, but makes little sense when one recognizes the property tax as a progressive levy borne predominantly by owners of capital.[10]

Second, the problems of the aged, or of households with temporarily depressed incomes, in paying property taxes should be met by tax deferral, not forgiveness. If temporary declines in income justify lightening tax burdens, temporary improvements would seem to justify raising them. Such a balanced approach would not subsidize fluctuating incomes at the expense of stable ones; but no circuit breaker embodies it. As another balancing technique, nonaged taxpayers could be granted the right to defer tax payments for a limited period, perhaps one or two years, and to make them up with interest over some relatively brief subsequent period. The plan might be exercisable at the taxpayer's option or might be limited to those who could show a decline in income. The aged might be permitted to defer payments indefinitely, with ultimate collection at the time the property is transferred by bequest, gift, or sale. A deferred plan along these lines was recently enacted in Massachusetts.[11] The state can handle financing of deferral, or make loans to subdivisions to relieve them of liquidity problems. In one sense, tax deferral alleviates temporary income declines or the hardships imposed on the aged more fully than does the circuit breaker, because it offers complete relief of current tax liability. Justifying tax forgiveness, in addition to tax deferral, requires some

10. One motivation for providing circuit-breaker relief for renters may rest on the accurate perception that owner-occupants already enjoy sizable tax advantages under the personal income tax and that additional tax relief for them should be accompanied by some sort of help to renters. The provisions of the personal income tax aiding homeowners are best understood, however, as favorable treatment of investment income. See Henry J. Aaron, *Shelter and Subsidies: Who Benefits from Federal Housing Policies?* (Brookings Institution, 1972), pp. 53–55.

11. Mary Thornton, "Property Tax Break for Elderly is Unfair to Others, Critics Say," *Boston Globe*, July 24, 1974. Under this law homeowners over the age of 65 who have lived in Massachusetts for at least ten years, owned their homes for five years, and have incomes of less than $20,000 a year can defer any part of property tax liabilities, provided that the accumulated deferrals do not exceed half of the assessed value of the property. When the owner dies or sells the property, the back taxes plus interest at 8 percent must be paid from the sale proceeds or directly by the heirs. Oregon, Texas, Virginia, and Utah have similar laws.

rationale for paying aid that rises with the wealth of the recipient, the paradox of most circuit breakers.

The force of the remaining objectives of circuit breakers are matters of judgment. It is questionable whether an indirect form of intrastate revenue sharing is necessary or desirable when all states have available such other means of aiding subdivisions as school aid and direct grants and when the federal government is directly aiding subdivisions through general and special revenue sharing. Whether circuit-breaker relief should be supported pending comprehensive income maintenance clearly depends in part on the efficiency with which it is targeted on needy households. Evidence on this question is scant; Bendick finds that in 1974, the Wisconsin circuit breaker, with a modest income limit of $7,000, directed 52 percent of all payments to the poor as measured by current annual income and reached 87 percent of all poor families and unrelated individuals.[12] Plans that lack income limits are less efficient.

An Alternative

Circuit breakers can be defended only as an interim form of income relief for the poor. Those who wish to pursue such a course should design a program that makes sense as income maintenance and deals with the problems property taxes can create for the aged or for those with temporarily depressed incomes. Such a program would have these two features: a simple system of grants to households related negatively to income and net worth; and provision for tax deferral, temporarily for the nonaged and until death for the aged.

First, a grant could be set equal to some fraction, f, of the expenditure, E, deemed necessary to purchase adequate housing, less some fraction, k, of income. For those wedded to the idea that property taxes are borne by tenants, f could be regarded as the proportion of housing expenditure "absorbed" by property taxes. Expenditure, E, would vary by family size, a feature absent from most circuit breakers. An illustrative formula, with E equal to $800, plus $200 times the number of household members (up to, say, six), f equal to 0.25, and k equal to 0.05, would provide the following benefits to a family of four at various incomes:

12. See Bendick, "Designing Circuit Breaker Property Tax Relief," pp. 26–27.

Income	Benefit
0	$400
$1,000	350
2,000	300
4,000	200
6,000	100
8,000	0

Second, if property taxes less these benefits (if any) exceed 5 percent of income, homeowners would be permitted to defer tax payments regardless of current income. For purposes of setting benefits, income should include intrafamily transfers and should pool the receipts of all household members; in addition, some fraction of net assets should be added to income or a net assets ceiling set.[13] The values of E, f, and k are purely illustrative and could be set at any level.

The chief advantages of this plan over conventional circuit breakers are that (1) benefits do not rise with wealth, (2) benefits do not rise with actual housing expenditures, and (3) the special problems of declines of current income below normal income are treated through an "averaging" device rather than through aid.

This approach is a considerable improvement over the older system of homestead exemptions, since it takes the income of the household into account in calculating aid. Although household expenditures are strongly correlated with normal income, the relationship is far from perfect. Not all owner-occupants of cheap housing have low incomes. Accordingly, homestead exemptions do not reach many low-income owner-occupants and simultaneously assist some households with ample means.

Reforming School Finance

Several state courts have ruled that existing methods of financing elementary and secondary education violate provisions of state constitutions and must be changed.[14] The difficulty with present arrangements is that, to raise equal amounts of revenue per pupil,

13. See ibid., p. 27, for similar proposed modifications in conventional circuit breakers.
14. For details, see Robert D. Reischauer and Robert W. Hartman, *Reforming School Finance* (Brookings Institution, 1973), especially pp. 58–59.

school districts with relatively small amounts of real property per pupil must impose much higher property tax rates than are necessary in districts endowed with large amounts of real property per pupil. Although all states compensate partly for these differences, the courts have held that some of these programs do not go far enough.[15]

In their search for constitutionally acceptable methods of financing education, state legislatures have considered a number of schemes, including increased state aid to school districts, state assumption of property taxation and equalization of rates, and "power equalization" under which aid formulas would be set to assure that a given effective property tax rate would yield each district the same amount of revenue per pupil.[16]

Most of these plans would bring about sizable changes in property tax rates among school districts and many would cause large reductions in average property taxes offset by commensurate increases in sales, income, or other taxes. Because property tax differentials are likely to be capitalized, these changes would cause major realignments in relative property values—increases in communities where property tax rates are cut, decreases where they are increased. For similar reasons, a shift away from property taxes will benefit owners in general through a rise in values. Efforts to reform school finance may well succeed in equalizing school expenditures, but in so doing will generate major windfall gains and losses for property owners.

Changing the Tax Base

Although never a comprehensive wealth tax, the property tax reached a sizable fraction of gross wealth in the era when farming was the principal economic activity.[17] Almost from the beginning, there have been moves to narrow the tax base by exempting specific

15. A number of decisions by state courts also have held that existing methods of school finance violate the United States Constitution, but the United States Supreme Court reversed these findings. See *Rodriguez* v. *San Antonio Independent School District*, reported in *New York Times*, March 21, 1973. This decision, however, does not overturn findings that the arrangements violate state constitutions.

16. See Reischauer and Hartman, *Reforming School Finance*, pp. 76–94.

17. For a history of the development of the property tax, see Jens Peter Jensen, *Property Taxation in the United States* (University of Chicago Press, 1931).

properties, by excluding certain forms of property (notably business inventories and personal property of businesses and individuals), or by restricting it to land. From a wholly different perspective, others have criticized the tax for not reaching all property and for not offsetting debts against assets, and have urged replacement of the property tax by a net wealth tax.

Real Property Exemptions

No one knows precisely how much real property is exempt from taxation. Netzer estimates that in 1966, $605 billion of tangible wealth was held by governments and tax-exempt organizations and that an additional $447 billion of property otherwise escaped taxation.[18] Balk reports a number of rough estimates that one-third of all real property in the United States is tax exempt.[19] If the ratios of tangible property to gross national product and of tax-exempt property to the total were the same in 1974 as Netzer estimated for 1966, $1,958 billion of the total $4,755 billion in tangible property was tax exempt in 1974.

The proportion of exempt property varies drastically among the states for a number of reasons. First, the proportion of property owned by the federal government or by religious organizations, exempt in all jurisdictions, varies widely. Second, some states also exempt property owned by cemeteries, medical facilities and hospitals, and fraternal, social, civic, and professional organizations. Third, nearly all states exempt parsonages and church-owned schools, but some also exempt all church-owned properties (motels, for example) if the income is used for religious and charitable activities, or if the property is being held for possible religious use.[20]

Considerable controversy surrounds the exemption of property on the basis of ownership. It has been argued that tax exemptions granted to owners with particular characteristics are equivalent to subsidy payments. The end result of taxing *A* and *B* each $100 and paying *B* a subsidy of $100 is the same as exempting *B* from the

18. Dick Netzer, "The Incidence of the Property Tax Revisited," *National Tax Journal*, vol. 26 (December 1973), p. 522.
19. Alfred Balk, *The Free List: Property without Taxes* (Russell Sage Foundation, 1971), pp. 10–19.
20. On the details of exemption practices, see ibid., especially the appendix, pp. 165–69.

tax and omitting the subsidy. On this theory, a New York taxpayer sued to deny tax exemptions to religious groups on the ground that they were equivalent to direct governmental grants to such groups, and that they violated constitutional provisions forbidding state financial support of organized religion.[21] The Supreme Court eventually held that the taxpayer's claim was invalid.[22]

The most persuasive argument against holding tax exemptions unconstitutional was advanced by Bittker, who pointed out that all taxes inevitably exempt something or someone:

There is no way to tax *everything;* a legislative body, no matter how avid for revenue, can do no more than pick out from the universe of people, entities, and events over which it has jurisdiction those that, in its view, are appropriate objects of taxation.[23]

The Supreme Court may have disposed of the challenge to the constitutionality of tax exemptions on property owned by religious organizations, but it could not resolve the political controversy over whether exemptions should be granted and, if so, to whom and by whom. In considering this question, treating tax exemptions *as if* they were grants combined with inclusive taxation helps clarify the desirability of exemptions.[24] Unless voters are willing to endorse (or reject) *both* (a) a system of exemptions *and* (b) a system of inclusive taxation combined with grants yielding the same distribution of income, their decisions may be inconsistent. In fact, exemptions and grants differ in one central political aspect: visibility. Exemptions, once granted, continue automatically or with only cursory review in most jurisdictions; in many, the value of the ex-

21. The case, *Walz* v. *Tax Commission of the City of New York,* alleged violations of the first and fourteenth amendments of the U.S. Constitution, as well as the New York constitution and real property tax laws. See Boris I. Bittker, "Churches, Taxes and the Constitution," *Yale Law Journal,* vol. 78 (July 1969), pp. 1285–1310.

22. See 397 U.S. 664.

23. Bittker, "Churches, Taxes and the Constitution," p. 1288. Bittker makes the point concrete by inquiring whether a 10 percent tax on admissions on all persons and corporations whose principal activity is the exhibition of motion pictures for profit is really a tax on (a) "frivolous expenditures, with 'exemptions' for . . . jewelry, perfume, and night clubs," (b) "methods of transmitting ideas, with 'exemptions' for newspapers, books, lending libraries, radio and television" (p. 1293), and so on, through three other classes of taxes and exemptions.

24. Stanley S. Surrey, *Pathways to Tax Reform: The Concept of Tax Expenditures* (Harvard University Press, 1973), especially pp. 1–49.

emption is unknown, since the tax-exempt property need not be listed or revalued periodically. The long-term cost of exemptions is unknown when they are enacted. Furthermore, the ultimate costs seldom appear explicitly in budgets, and the issuance of exemptions requires only the administrative determination that the applicant qualifies under law. By contrast, a system of grants would be subject to periodic scrutiny by state or local legislators, because the cost would appear annually (or at least biennially) in budgets.

A case can be made for insulating tax exemptions from the uncertainties of annual legislative action through the use of broad authorities. Without such insulation, legislators might be tempted to compel individual property owners to accede to particular policies by threatening to withdraw exemptions. But this insulation does not require that exemptions be specified in state constitutions, thereby vastly complicating any efforts to reexamine them. Nor does it require that legislators blind themselves to the current market value of exempt properties and to the cost of exempting them.[25] Lacking such data, legislators cannot know whether exemptions continue to serve the community's interests.

The case against valuation of exempt property contains three major elements. First, in many cases, such an exercise is highly arbitrary: What is the market value of Harvard Yard or the Statue of Liberty? Second, money spent to administer a tax that is not going to be collected is money wasted.[26] Third, the value of activities carried out by exempt organizations often vastly exceeds the tax forgone on exempt property.

The first two arguments are related, and both suggest that only limited resources should be devoted to valuation of exempt properties, especially those that are hard to appraise. Rough estimates that would not suffice for assigning tax burdens are likely to be adequate for deciding whether to perpetuate existing exemptions— especially since, as the third argument suggests, legislators will often

25. Only fourteen of the thirty-nine states (plus the District of Columbia) responding to a Senate survey reported that they regularly make and publish assessments of exempt property. See *Status of Property Tax Administration in the States*, Prepared by the Subcommittee on Intergovernmental Relations of the Senate Committee on Government Operations, 93 Cong. 1 sess. (1973), p. 16.

26. See Dick Netzer, "Property Tax Exemptions and Their Effects: A Dissenting View," in National Tax Association, *1972 Proceedings of the Sixty-Fifth Annual Conference on Taxation* (1973), pp. 268–74.

conclude that exemptions yield services far more valuable than the revenues forgone. However, the contention that property tax exemptions are frequently the cheapest—indeed, the only—subsidy available to localities or states to sustain private provision of services that the public would otherwise have to furnish (and at greater cost) is an argument for continuing specific exemptions, not against the valuation of exempt property. The "wasted-money" argument against up-to-date appraisals on exempt property must be weighed against the continuing need for such information for legislative purposes.[27]

Furthermore, exemptions, usually initiated at the state level, reduce revenues of localities, thereby enabling one level of government—the state—to reap the political gains from responding to pleas for relief, while another—the locality—pays the cost. In general, the system by which exemptions are granted and extended in most states seems almost deliberately designed to promote irresponsible legislative behavior.[28]

The practice of awarding property tax exemptions could be purged of existing shortcomings if (1) constitutional provisions requiring exemption of specific kinds of property were repealed; (2) legislatures were empowered by state constitutions to award exemptions for specific periods on any class of property; (3) appraisers were required to value exempt properties, and the cost of exemptions in terms of revenue forgone were included in the budget of each government granting an exemption. Even if all these steps were taken, one shortcoming of exemptions would remain: owners of exempt property are encouraged to use more property than would appear optimal if they had to pay property taxes. Since this particular subsidy is available in proportion to the use of real estate but not of other factors of production, schools and universities, hospitals, other property owners, and cities themselves are en-

27. For recommendations along these lines, see the Advisory Commission on Intergovernmental Relations, *The Role of the States in Strengthening the Property Tax* (ACIR, 1963). For more recent discussion of the same views and recommendations for reform, see Balk, *Free List*, pp. 127–45; and "The Erosion of the Ad Valorem Real Estate Tax Base," Report of the Property Taxation Committee, printed in *Tax Policy*, vol. 40, no. 1 (1973).

28. In addition to better data on the cost of exemptions and payments by states to localities to cover them, Balk calls for charging exempt organizations fees for specific community services. See *Free List*, pp. 127–45.

couraged to produce their services by methods that are more real estate–intensive than would otherwise be desirable. University and college campuses, for example, are probably larger than they would be if administrators counted in their budgets the property taxes that would be collectable from other owners.[29] This problem inheres in property tax exemptions and suggests that they should be used only when other instruments for providing subsidies are constitutionally prohibited or politically unacceptable.[30]

Preferential Taxation of Farmers

More than half the states (thirty in January 1973) provide special exemptions for farmland, similar to those first offered in Maryland in 1956. These laws require the valuation of farmland for tax purposes, not according to market value, but according to its agricultural use. The intent is to shield farmers near growing urban centers from the rise in taxes on rapidly appreciating land prices. Because they could not afford such taxes out of farm income, it is alleged that they would be driven to sell land to developers and speculators who would aggravate urban sprawl. Elderly farmers would be forced off the land at an age when they could not easily pursue another profession. Thus, farmland exemptions are justified as a device to limit the social and human costs of unplanned growth.

The nature of the exemptions varies. Some states defer taxation on the difference between market value and value as farmland for a number of years or until the land is sold. At time of sale, all or part of the deferred taxes are collected, but in no case is the owner required to pay full interest on them. Other states give preferential treatment to farmers, but do not bother to collect additional taxes later. Still others enter into specific agreements under which the state or locality reduces taxes if the owner accepts certain restrictions on the use of his land for a stipulated period. In practice, these agreements amount to preferred assessment.

If capital markets operated perfectly, none of these arrangements

29. For a recommendation that currently exempt owners be subject to a tax on land, but not on improvements, see Oliver Oldman and Ferdinand P. Schoettle, *State and Local Taxes, and Finances: Text, Problems and Cases* (Foundation Press, 1974), p. 345, where C. K. Cobb, Jr., is quoted and advocates taxation of land for currently exempt owners.

30. I am indebted to Dick Netzer for suggesting this point. See his "Property Tax Exemptions and their Effects."

would be required. Farmers whose land was becoming more valuable would be able to borrow against their appreciating asset to cover any taxes for which the proceeds from farming were insufficient. They would retain ownership and perhaps continue farming until they concluded that the present value of proceeds from sale less any tax loans had reached a maximum. In practice, loans may be unavailable or unduly costly, and farm owners may respond by selling too soon and miss capital gains they could have earned by waiting longer. The purchaser still has every incentive to defer final development until the present value of the land has reached a maximum. For this reason, it is not clear why the property tax should lead to premature development. Concessions to farmers adopted so far plainly have the effect of postponing development by requiring that developed uses pay a higher tax than does farming. Such a policy can be justified only if other actions of government or economic imperfections balance it by encouraging premature development.

In the absence of evidence supporting artificial deferral, special farmland exemptions are inequitable and should be repealed. They specifically reduce taxes for owners of a rapidly appreciating asset and, hence, rapidly growing wealth. Even the plans that ostensibly defer taxes in fact reduce them. Genuine deferral would require that deferred taxes be accumulated at market interest as a permanent lien against the property. The justification could be the same as that for the Massachusetts plan allowing deferral for aged homeowners: farmers should be permitted readily to use equity in their farmland to pay current tax liabilities. However, unlike the situation facing the aged, there is no indication that surburban land is an illiquid asset, that farmers as a class are unwilling to farm land owned by others, or that they are unable to negotiate bank loans. If state governments conclude that development surrounding urban areas should be restricted, instruments of direct control are at hand. If owners are restricted from development at the time they choose to undertake it, compensation is due and property taxes should be cut, but current farmland exemptions are poorly designed for this purpose.

Personal Property Taxation

The taxation of household tangible personal property customarily is achieved through specific treatment of certain commodities, such as automobiles. Most of the few states that do not completely exempt household personal property allow localities to exclude it from the tax base.[31] The equitable taxation of tangible personal property of households requires physical entry into dwelling units and sizable administrative costs. Furthermore, many kinds of property, such as jewelry, art objects, and small appliances, are concealed easily. The gains in economic efficiency from removing a tax differential that favors personal over real property do not warrant the costs of taxing personal property equitably. Except for easily taxed items such as automobiles, the pretense should be abandoned.

The case against taxing intangible personal property is even stronger. It can be concealed even more easily from local administrators, not only physically, but also financially, behind trusts. Furthermore, such taxation imposes a double tax on business property that is directly taxed. A bond floated to pay for a factory would be subject to tax on a base initially equal in value to the building and machinery that the bond financed and that were independently taxed. Thirty-four states and the District of Columbia make no effort to tax intangible personal property.

Business personal property is treated in various ways. Most states tax machinery. But a growing number exempt business inventories in whole or in part. Like household personal property, inventories can be concealed, by keeping them outside the taxing jurisdiction or by depletion just before the valuation date. In some jurisdictions some retail stores schedule bargain sales to achieve this objective. In either case, the tax can lead businesses to make decisions unjustifiable on any other grounds. Taxing authorities can mitigate these effects only by basing the tax on average annual inventories. Such information could be obtained through sales or income tax returns, but few states have attempted to get it. On balance, it seems preferable to repeal the tax on business personal property.

Land Taxation

Land taxation has enjoyed support for two independent reasons. At least since Henry George advocated it in 1879, appreciation in

31. The valuation of personal property is a joke. New Mexico, for example, sets the value of household personal property arbitrarily at 10 percent of the taxable value of the home, a procedure that is equivalent to raising the residential property tax by 10 percent and leaving household personal property exempt.

land values has been held fit for taxation because such gains are created socially, not by the efforts of their owners.[32] In addition, economists have favored land taxation as perhaps the only practical major tax available that does not distort economic decisions.[33] A land tax would not fall on improvements, and unlike the conventional real property tax, it would not deter any investment whose gross returns exceed costs.

Whether the property tax should be replaced by a land-value tax involves both theoretical and practical considerations. The case against an *abrupt* replacement of the property tax by a land-value tax is overwhelming, for it would entail massive redistributions of tax burdens, as well as major shifts in property values.[34] Despite the emotional effusions on the ethical primacy of land values as a tax base, the ethical appeal of such redistributions of property values is difficult to perceive. The most that can be said for such injustices is that they might be defensible if required to achieve the goal of reducing distortions caused by real property taxes. But they are not necessary, because a tax freeze, followed by equal percentage adjustments to meet changing revenue needs, would accomplish the objective. Such a tax would end investment distortions as effectively as would the land tax, because the return from new investments would not suffer at all. Moreover, unlike a shift to land taxation, this method would not redistribute tax burdens. Such a tax would enjoy no legitimacy, however, because some currently valuable properties might later depreciate so that taxes on them would exceed their value and because it would bear even less

32. See Peter M. Mieszkowski, "A Critical Appraisal of Land Value Taxation," (University of Houston, May 1970; processed); and Dick Netzer, *The Economics of the Property Tax* (Brookings Institution, 1966), pp. 197–212.

33. See chap. 3. A small amount of revenue might be raised through head taxes, but they are regarded universally as deeply inequitable since they, like Anatole France's law against sleeping under bridges, fall with cool impartiality on rich and poor alike.

34. For example, assume that the ratio of the value of land to improvements averages 0.25, and that effective property tax rates average 2 percent. If two properties with equal assessed values have ratios of land value to total value of 0.1 and 0.5, respectively, a switch from the conventional property tax to a land-value tax will decrease taxes by 60 percent on the first, and increase property taxes by 100 percent on the second. Given full capitalization at 10 percent, the price of the first property would rise by 12 percent while that of the second fell by 20 percent. This calculation disregards the impact on land values of changes in the demand for land induced by the change in taxation.

relation to benefits received by property owners than does the current one. For this reason, a tax freeze is as much of a curiosity as is an abrupt shift to land taxation.

Even if the switch were gradual, site valuation is still subject to criticism because its basic premise, that the supply of sites is fixed, is not correct. Quite apart from the minor point that new sites are created through landfill, grading, and development of air rights, any practical land tax would be imposed by jurisdictions with limited boundaries. When such jurisdictions are bordered by annexable land not subject to taxation—a characteristic of most urban areas —the supply of sites to their residents is elastic. A land-value tax will have specific effects tending to limit the extent of the city.[35] As Mieszkowski writes:

At least part of this favorable effect [of a land-value tax] will be offset in the longer run if LVT is restricted to urban areas. Agricultural uses for land compete with urban uses. If LVT is restricted to urban uses, and if the supply of undeveloped agricultural land to urban areas is perfectly elastic at a given price, the imposition of a LVT will eventually increase the effective cost of urban land (including the tax) by the amount of the tax, for if additional rural land is to be brought into urban use it will have to sell at its value in agriculture. Although the price of raw land is only a fraction of the cost of developed urban land, the imposition of LVT on developed land is equivalent to taxing a proportion of improvements.[36]

When the taxing jurisdiction is completely surrounded by sites that cannot be annexed, so that its size is fixed, changes in land-value taxes would not affect its size nor, hence, the number of sites it contains. These facts characterize most central cities and suggest that the advantages of land taxes are likely to be greater there than in surrounding suburbs.

If all jurisdictions reduced property taxes by the same number of percentage points and raised land taxes enough to hold revenues

35. Thus, let P_r be the annual rental value of undeveloped rural land surrounding the taxing jurisdiction and t the tax rate as a fraction of annual rental value, P_d, of land within the jurisdiction. If land values decrease as one moves out from the center of the taxing jurisdiction, it will extend to the point where $(1 - t)P_d = P_r$. For analysis of the effects of property taxes on city size, deduced within a fully articulated model of an urban economy with taxes and public services, see A. Mitchell Polinsky and Daniel L. Rubinfeld, "The Long Run Incidence of a Residential Property Tax and Local Public Services," Working Paper 1207-29 (Urban Institute, 1974; processed).

36. "Critical Appraisal of Land Value Taxation," p. 14.

unchanged, the relative ability of various communities to bid for reproducible capital would not be affected, since the *difference* in taxes levied on such capital would be unchanged. If, however, one jurisdiction reduced taxes on improvements more than others did, it would be able to compete more effectively for capital.

This elementary fact of interjurisdictional tax competition has not escaped city planners and tax assessors. They have recognized it, however, not by replacing the property tax with a land tax, but by awarding reduced tax rates to investors contemplating sites within the jurisdiction. Such special arrangements can be framed to offer investors most of the advantages that the general exemption of improvements would bring, but the retention of the property tax for current residents avoids the sizable reallocation of tax burdens, and hence, the major shifts in capital values among them that a shift to land taxation would entail.

In summary, an abrupt shift to land taxation would cause widespread and capricious redistributions of taxes and land values to achieve a goal that can be reached with fewer distortions by freezing existing property taxes. Even a freeze would cause shifts in land values because investors now believe taxes will rise more on properties expected to appreciate rapidly than on those expected to appreciate slowly, and these expected taxes affect current valuation. Until economists not only argue that economic efficiency will improve if land taxation is adopted but also show the order of magnitude of these gains, they will be in no position to urge upon taxpayers the readjustments that such a shift would entail.

Net-Worth Tax

Certain inequities are inherent in the property tax. It falls predominantly on gross holdings of real property, not on net holdings or on equities. These features mean that taxpayers with equal net worth probably face different property tax liabilities. For this reason, critics of the property tax correctly observe that it is poorly correlated with accepted measures of ability to pay.

One remedy for this shortcoming would be to replace the property tax with a net-worth tax, levied periodically on the total assets less the total liabilities of each taxable unit. Thurow has argued that a net-worth tax is a desirable component of any tax system based on ability to pay.[37] He reasons that households in attempting to maximize their own welfare will adjust their net worth, through saving or dissaving, until the marginal value of an additional dollar of net worth just equals the marginal value of current consumption. For this reason, he argues, the two bases—consumption and net worth—both must be taxed if the tax system is to rest on well-being as evaluated by each household. This argument, however, is invalid. If net worth is eventually consumed, it would be taxed by the consumption tax. If net worth is held until death, it should be treated as consumption at that time. In any case, Thurow's argument suggests a tax on *additions* to net worth, not on net worth itself.

An older and more persuasive argument for taxing net worth relies on the contention that individuals enjoy benefits from the possession of net assets quite independent from the eventual consumption or bequests that those assets will become. These benefits incude economic and political power, and form a fair base for taxation.

A net-worth tax, however, could be administered only at the national level, because it could be evaded easily if lower-level governments imposed significant rates. It could not, therefore, serve the political function performed by the property tax as the principal revenue source of local governments. Furthermore, a net-worth tax would quite likely be set aside on the ground that it violates the constitutional prohibition against direct taxes apportioned among the states except according to population. Whatever the other reasons for its appeal, the net-worth tax cannot be regarded as a substitute for the property tax in the United States.

37. Lester C. Thurow, *The Impact of Taxes on the American Economy* (Praeger, 1971), pp. 122–24.

CHAPTER SIX

Summary and Prospects

THE PROPERTY TAX comprises a wide variety of taxes levied at different rates on variously defined bases; administrative efficiency ranges from atrocious to excellent. Administration of the tax improved, at least until 1966, as measured by the most commonly used index, the coefficient of dispersion, though the meaningfulness of this measure is open to considerable doubt.

The property tax has been, and is likely to remain, the mainstay of local government finance. Although the receipts from other taxes have grown more rapidly, the proportion of gross national product collected as property taxes rose until 1972 (but has diminished somewhat since then). In general, those states in which the fraction of state and local revenues collected through property taxes is highest reduced their relative reliance on them during the sixties. Furthermore, property taxes constitute larger fractions of state and local revenues in those states that leave educational finance disproportionately to localities. The relative importance of the tax seems likely to diminish if states assume an increasing share of the costs of elementary and secondary education.

Opinions about the desirability of reliance on the property tax are heavily influenced by opinions about its incidence. The prevailing view outside the economics profession holds that the property tax is a kind of excise tax on the users of commodities produced by taxable real property. Thus, renters are thought to bear property taxes levied on their residences, just as automobile owners bear the taxes levied on the factories that produce cars and the materials they embody. Since consumption expenditures in general, and housing expenditures in particular, are a larger fraction of low than of high incomes, the property tax is widely regarded as regressive.

Recent economic analysis suggests that this view is incomplete on at least two grounds. First, the property tax is not primarily an excise on consumers, but rather a tax on capital; the burdens of the property tax are shared by all owners of capital. Since the ownership of capital, or net worth, is progressively distributed with respect to income, the property tax on balance is a progressive, not a regressive, tax. Additional losses (or gains) may be suffered (or enjoyed) by workers or landowners or consumers who reside in communities with tax rates above (or below) the average, or who consume commodities subject to especially heavy (or light) taxes. However, these excise-tax effects are quite unlikely to reverse, and are more likely to reinforce, the progressivity of that part of the burden of the property tax that is distributed among owners of capital.

A second reason for rejecting the view that the property tax is regressive is the questionable practice of classifying households for incidence analysis by annual income. This practice can make even a progressive tax seem regressive. Correcting for this source of bias by averaging household incomes over periods longer than one year suggests that the property tax is proportional or progressive throughout most of the income distribution.

The importance of this revision in analysis of tax incidence for evaluating the property tax can hardly be exaggerated. Indeed, the tax becomes one of the more progressive elements in the national tax system rather than one of the most regressive. In the light of the growing importance of the regressive payroll tax and the diminishing importance of the progressive corporation income tax, the distributional pattern of the property tax has considerable impact on estimates of the distribution of burdens imposed by the U.S. tax system as a whole.[1] Advocates of greater progressivity in the system should recognize that the property tax advances rather than obstructs achievement of egalitarian objectives.

1. Compare the estimates shown in tables 3-1 and 3-5.

Evaluation of the property tax, however, cannot rest solely on considerations of distribution among income classes. Inept and fragmented administration imposes unequal burdens on households in otherwise identical circumstances. Some variations in tax burdens, especially those that arose long ago, may have been capitalized into sales prices, so that their correction today would introduce new inequities. But capricious or clumsy administration introduces new inequities continuously, especially when relative property values change rapidly. Furthermore, bad administration deprives the property tax of legitimacy among taxpayers. Administrative tools are at hand, and are being introduced in some jurisdictions, that permit frequent and accurate revaluation with fewer costly on-site inspections. Providing full information on assessment methods and on opportunities for quick, cheap appeals by disgruntled taxpayers can help legitimize the property tax. To achieve such reforms, very small assessing jurisdictions must be eliminated.

However well the property tax may be administered, and however clearly its basic progressivity comes to be understood, some taxpayers—especially aged homeowners, and younger homeowners with temporarily depressed incomes—will still have tax bills that are large relative to their current incomes. While economists tend to argue that this predicament is a signal that the taxpayer is over-housed, legislators have been loath to agree that the aged, the sick, or the temporarily unemployed should be compelled to move because they live in "more" house than their current incomes justify. They have responded instead by enacting homestead exemptions for the aged and, recently, "circuit breakers"—various devices to relieve property owners whose tax burdens are deemed to be excessive. Circuit breakers are inefficient because they target most aid within each income class on households with the greatest wealth. A system that allows deferral of tax liabilities, combined with cash assistance based on income, would allow the aged, and those with temporarily depressed incomes, to retain their homes without introducing undesirable incentives into the tax system.

Legislatures have been asked to modify the property tax in a variety of other ways. A broad spectrum of religious, educational, and other organizations have requested and received exemptions from property taxation. In some cases, such exemptions are efficient instruments by which the public, with a minimum of entanglement, can subsidize services that otherwise would have to be provided collectively. In many cases, the public purpose served by exemptions is obscure. However defensible the purpose of the exemptions, in few instances do authorities awarding them have adequate information on their cost, particularly those granted long ago. The process by which exemptions are awarded and perpetuated requires a drastic overhaul involving attempts at valuation, periodic review of the exemption both in principle and in amount, and assignment of the burden of the exemption to the level of government that grants it.

The practice of granting a variety of tax concessions to owners of rapidly appreciating farmland surrounding expanding metropolitan areas is particularly questionable. This device provides an additional boon to the owners of a valuable and appreciating asset at the expense of other, perhaps less lucky, taxpayers. While deferral of taxes on such land may be desirable to protect those who wish to continue farming from experiencing unfavorable cash flow, the deferred taxes, accumulated at market interest rates, should be recovered when the farmland is sold.

For many years economists have urged the exemption of improvements to real property from taxation, thus converting the property tax into a land tax. They have held that, unlike a tax on improvements, a land tax would not distort investment behavior by discouraging some otherwise profitable investments. Whatever its theoretical appeal, the substitution of a land tax would cause such enormous and arbitrary shifts in tax burdens and in property values that a swift and complete switch is unthinkable. A gradual switch would soften these effects. However, the argument that the land tax is nondistorting is flawed because the application of the tax at different rates by numerous jurisdictions, particularly at the edge of growing metropolitan areas, will affect the pace of urban expansion and development.

The foregoing analysis of tax incidence and of proposals for reform implies that the property tax will remain a major local tax for the foreseeable future; that its perpetuation should not disturb those anxious to maintain or to enhance the progressivity of the U.S. tax system; and that much legitimate discontent about the tax is explained by bad administration, which can be improved with tools at hand. Furthermore, most of the reforms enacted or

proposed to improve the equity of the property tax or to counter
its allegedly harmful effects turn out on close examination to be
questionable themselves.

Details on Results Reported
in Tables 3-3 and 3-6

Table 3-3

THE FULL results of the regressions summarized in table 3-3 are presented below. The variables are denoted as follows:

Y_1 = logarithm of 1971 rent
Y_2 = logarithm of property tax rate, renters
Y_3 = logarithm of property tax, renters
Y_4 = logarithm of 1971 home value
Y_5 = logarithm of property tax rate, homeowners
Y_6 = logarithm of property tax, homeowners
X_1 = logarithm of permanent total income (weighted)
X_2 = dummy variable; 1 if nonwhite; 0 otherwise
X_3, X_4, X_5, X_6 = dummy variables, for size of largest city in primary sampling unit, a Census Bureau category. All variables are zero unless the largest city has a population of 500,000 or more, in which case $X_3 = 1$; if the largest city has a population of 100,000 to 500,000, $X_4 = 1$; if the largest city has a population of 50,000 to 99,999, $X_5 = 1$; if the largest city has a population of 25,000 to 49,999, $X_6 = 1$
X_7, X_8, X_9 = dummy variables for distance from nearest city with population of 50,000 or more. All variables are zero unless the distance is less than five miles, in which case $X_7 = 1$; if the distance is 5 to 14.9 miles, $X_8 = 1$; if the distance is 15 to 29.9 miles, $X_9 = 1$
X_{10}, X_{11}, X_{12} = dummy variables for region of country. All variables are zero, unless region is the Northeast, in which case $X_{10} = 1$; if region is North Central, $X_{11} = 1$; if the region is the South, $X_{12} = 1$

X_{13}, X_{14}, X_{15}, X_{16}, X_{17} = dummy variables for family status. All variables
are zero if the family unit is a single person; $X_{13} = 1$ if the family
unit is a couple; $X_{14} = 1$ if the family unit is a single person with one
to three children; $X_{15} = 1$ if the family unit is a couple with one to
three children; $X_{16} = 1$ if the family unit is a single person with four
or more children; $X_{17} = 1$ if the family unit is a couple with four or
more children

X_{18} = dummy variable; 1 if the family reported savings of any amount;
0 otherwise

X_{19} = dummy variable; 1 if the family reported savings equal to at least two
months' income; 0 otherwise

X_{20} = dummy variable; 1 if the family reported owning a business; 0
otherwise

X_{21}, X_{22}, X_{23}, X_{24} = dummy variables for labor force status. All variables
are zero if the head worked 40 or more weeks in 1970; if the head is
currently working or unemployed *and* worked fewer than 40 weeks
in 1970, $X_{21} = 1$; if the head is retired or permanently disabled *and*
worked fewer than 40 weeks in 1970, $X_{22} = 1$; if the head is a house-
wife *and* worked fewer than 40 weeks in the previous year, $X_{23} = 1$;
if the head is a student *and* worked fewer than 40 weeks in 1970,
$X_{24} = 1$

X_{25} = logarithm of permanent income weighted (same as X_1, but with
windfalls excluded).

In the following regressions, the numbers in parentheses are *t*-values.

Regression Results

(1) $Y_1 = 2.23 + 0.561 X_1.$
        (4.75) (10.39)

$$\bar{R}^2 = 0.3220; \quad N = 226.$$

(2) $Y_2 = 0.607 + 0.009 X_1.$
        (1.22)   (0.15)

$$\bar{R}^2 = -0.0044; \quad N = 226.$$

(3) $Y_3 = 0.351 + 0.569 X_1.$
        (0.45)   (6.38)

$$\bar{R}^2 = 0.1501; \quad N = 226.$$

(4a) $Y_1 = 3.98 + 0.336 X_{25} + 0.117 X_2 - 0.116 X_{11} - 0.207 X_{12}$
        (7.70) (5.30)   (2.01)   (-1.79)   (-3.67)

$\quad + 0.072 X_{13} + 0.225 X_{14} + 0.201 X_{15} + 0.317 X_{16} + 0.372 X_{17}$
$\quad\quad (0.81)\quad\quad (2.85)\quad\quad (2.83)\quad\quad (2.90)\quad\quad (3.02)$

$$+ 0.202X_{18} + 0.288X_{19} + 0.246X_{20} - 0.252X_{21}.$$
$$(3.38) \qquad (3.83) \qquad (2.00) \qquad (-3.85)$$
$$\bar{R}^2 = 0.4551; \qquad N = 226.$$

(4b) $\quad Y_1 = 3.46 + 0.336X_1 + 0.264X_2 + 0.371X_3 + 0.118X_4$
$$(6.18) \ (5.26) \qquad (4.29) \qquad (1.59) \qquad (0.50)$$

$$+ 0.080X_5 + 0.512X_6 + 0.106X_7 + 0.184X_8 - 0.031X_9$$
$$(0.34) \qquad (1.54) \qquad (0.76) \qquad (1.35) \qquad (-0.21)$$

$$- 0.017X_{10} - 0.133X_{11} - 0.145X_{12} + 0.174X_{13} + 0.280X_{14}$$
$$(-0.14) \qquad (-2.07) \qquad (-2.57) \qquad (2.01) \qquad (3.54)$$

$$+ 0.234X_{15} + 0.299X_{16} + 0.385X_{17} + 0.170X_{18} + 0.225X_{19}$$
$$(3.36) \qquad (2.66) \qquad (3.20) \qquad (2.82) \qquad (3.08)$$

$$+ 0.237X_{20} - 0.193X_{21} - 0.064X_{22} + 0.102X_{23} - 0.079X_{24}.$$
$$(2.01) \qquad (-2.88) \qquad (0.54) \qquad (1.04) \qquad (-0.59)$$
$$\bar{R}^2 = 0.5185; \qquad N = 226.$$

(5) $\quad Y_2 = 0.911 - 0.004X_{25} - 0.158X_{11} - 0.499X_{12} + 0.0204X_{13}.$
$$(2.09) \quad (-0.076) \quad (-2.44) \quad (-8.98) \quad (0.27)$$
$$\bar{R}^2 = 0.2585; \qquad N = 226.$$

(6) $\quad Y_3 = 1.238 + 0.491X_{25} - 0.064X_2 - 0.286X_{11} - 0.718X_{12}$
$$(1.68) \quad (5.62) \qquad (-0.73) \quad (-2.74) \quad (-7.97)$$

$$- 0.024X_{13} + 0.204X_{18} + 0.329X_{19}.$$
$$(-0.19) \quad (2.21) \qquad (2.83)$$
$$\bar{R}^2 = 0.3500; \qquad N = 226.$$

(7a) $\quad Y_4 = -0.801 + 1.13X_1.$
$$(-1.06) \quad (13.75)$$
$$\bar{R}^2 = 0.4961; \qquad N = 192.$$

(7b) $\quad Y_4 = -0.932 + 1.15X_{25}.$
$$(-1.22) \quad (13.77)$$
$$\bar{R}^2 = 0.4968; \qquad N = 192$$

(8) $\quad Y_5 = -0.522 + 0.114X_1.$
$$(-0.81) \quad (1.62)$$
$$\bar{R}^2 = 0.0085; \qquad N = 192.$$

(9a) $\quad Y_6 = -5.928 + 1.246X_1.$
$$(-5.64) \quad (10.85)$$
$$\bar{R}^2 = 0.3792; \qquad N = 192.$$

(9b) $Y_6 = -6.402 + 1.302X_{25}.$
        (-6.13) (11.38)

$$\bar{R}^2 = 0.4020; \quad N = 192.$$

(10a) $Y_4 = -0.322 + 0.995X_1 + 0.701X_7 + 0.666X_8 + 0.636X_9$
        (-0.40) (10.43) (5.22) (5.42) (4.05)

        $+\; 0.148X_{13} + 0.282X_{14} + 0.213X_{15} + 0.283X_{16} + 0.249X_{17}$
        $\quad(0.86)$ $\quad(1.25)$ $\quad(1.29)$ $\quad(1.17)$ $\quad(1.35)$

        $+\; 0.284X_{20}.$
        $\quad(2.06)$

$$\bar{R}^2 = 0.5676; \quad N = 192.$$

(10b) $Y_4 = 0.210 + 0.907X_1 + 0.118X_2 + 0.165X_6 + 0.536X_7$
        (0.20) (7.33) (1.00) (0.93) (2.95)

        $+\; 0.523X_8 + 0.495X_9 - 0.035X_{10} - 0.074X_{11} - 0.045X_{12}$
        $\quad(3.07)$ $\quad(2.64)$ $\quad(-0.17)$ $\quad(-0.56)$ $\quad(-0.35)$

        $+\; 0.230X_{13} + 0.393X_{14} + 0.331X_{15} + 0.355X_{16} + 0.437X_{17}$
        $\quad(1.26)$ $\quad(1.57)$ $\quad(1.91)$ $\quad(1.31)$ $\quad(2.10)$

        $+\; 0.130X_{18} + 0.166X_{19} + 0.270X_{20} + 0.055X_{21} + 0.030X_{22}$
        $\quad(0.97)$ $\quad(1.19)$ $\quad(1.85)$ $\quad(0.36)$ $\quad(0.16)$

        $+\; 0.470X_{23} - 0.499X_{24}.$
        $\quad(1.50)$ $\quad(-1.35)$

$$\bar{R}^2 = 0.5611; \quad N = 192.$$

(11) $Y_5 = 0.640 + 0.013X_1 + 0.514X_{10} - 0.143X_{11} - 0.545X_{12}.$
        (1.14) (0.21) (3.72) (-1.51) (-5.96)

$$\bar{R}^2 = 0.3208; \quad N = 192.$$

(12a) $Y_6 = -4.842 + 1.077X_1 + 0.929X_7 + 0.843X_8$
        (5.04) (10.39) (5.82) (5.49)

        $+\; 0.776X_9 + 0.550X_{10} - 0.145X_{11} - 0.562X_{12}.$
        $\quad(3.95)$ $\quad(2.34)$ $\quad(-0.91)$ $\quad(-3.57)$

$$\bar{R}^2 = 0.5507; \quad N = 192.$$

(12b) $Y_6 = -5.09 + 1.115X_{25} + 0.868X_7 + 0.774X_8 + 0.693X_9$
        (-5.31) (10.69) (5.49) (5.06) (3.54)

        $+\; 0.528X_{10} - 0.124X_{11} - 0.573X_{12}.$
        $\quad(2.27)$ $\quad(-0.79)$ $\quad(-3.69)$

$$\bar{R}^2 = 0.5602; \quad N = 192.$$

Illustration of Excise-Tax Effects

To illustrate the importance of excise-tax effects, I created a hypothetical world of nine cities with an aggregate population of 9,600. Each city contained five income classes, with average incomes of $1,000, $5,000, $10,000, $20,000, and $50,000, respectively (table A-1). The relative size of each in-

Table A-1. Population Distribution by Average Income, and Property Tax Rate, Cities in Hypothetical World

Average income (dollars)	City									Total
	1	2	3	4	5	6	7	8	9	
					Population					
1,000	190	170	150	130	120	90	70	50	30	1,000
5,000	370	340	310	280	250	220	190	160	130	2,250
10,000	400	400	400	400	400	400	400	400	400	3,600
20,000	130	160	190	220	250	280	310	340	370	2,250
50,000	10	20	35	45	50	65	75	90	110	500
Total	1,100	1,090	1,085	1,075	1,070	1,055	1,045	1,040	1,040	9,600
				Property tax rate (percent)						
	1	3	5	2	4	6	3	5	7	4

Source: Hypothetical world devised for illustrative purposes. See accompanying text.

Table A-2. Income, Assets, and Consumption per Household by Economic Class, Hypothetical World

Dollars

Economic class	Average income	Assets	Consumption
A	1,000	1,000	2,500
B	5,000	7,500	6,000
C	10,000	22,500	10,000
D	20,000	67,500	16,000
E	50,000	255,000	32,000

Source: Same as table A-1.

come class varied among the cities so that average income varied from $8,309 to $16,904. Arbitrary property tax rates were assigned to each city; most of the variation in rates was random, but higher-income cities were assigned somewhat higher rates. Associated with each household in each income class were stipulated asset holdings and consumption expenditures (table A-2). The income elasticity of asset holdings was set at approximately 1.5 and that of consumption at approximately 0.6. None of the values of the relevant variables presented in tables A-1 and A-2 is meant to be descriptive of the actual distribution of population, income, assets, consumption, or property tax rates. They are intended, rather, to explore the range of possible excise-tax effects in a world where these effects are at least as large as in the real world.

Following the new view of property tax incidence, I divided the burden into two parts, one flowing from the average tax rate, $\bar{t}$, defined as

$$\bar{t} = \frac{\sum_i \sum_j A_{ij} t_j}{\sum_i \sum_j A_{ij}},$$

where A_{ij} is the asset holdings of income bracket i in city j and t_j is the tax rate in city j; and the other flowing from deviations in the tax rate of a particular city around the average Δt_j where $\Delta t_j = t_j - \bar{t}$. The first part was defined for each bracket as

$$\frac{\sum_i \sum_j A_{ij} \bar{t}}{\sum_i \sum_j Y_{ij}},$$

where Y_{ij} is the income in income bracket i in city j. This expression may be written more simply as

$$\frac{\bar{t} \bar{A}_k}{\bar{Y}_k},$$

where $\bar{A}_k$ and $\bar{Y}_k$ are the average assets and income of each person in income bracket k. The excise-tax effects, which may be positive or negative for each income bracket and which sum to zero for all brackets, are assumed to result from higher (or lower) product prices for citizens of the cities with higher (or lower) property taxes. The excise tax effect for each income bracket in each city is

$$\left[\frac{\sum_i \Delta t_j A_{ij}}{\sum_i C_{ij}} \right] C_{ij},$$

where C_{ij} is consumption by income bracket in city j. The illustration makes no allowance for tax exporting to consumers in other cities, for shifting of burdens to landowners through lower land prices, or for shifting of burdens to labor through lower wages. Were these factors to be built into the calculations, they would reduce the magnitude of the excise-tax effects. Tax exporting would distribute the effects of high (low) taxes, now focused predominantly on upper- (lower-) income households, among a broader sample of the population. The shifting of tax burdens to landowners and workers would reduce the need for changes in prices of final products. For these reasons, the illustration almost certainly overstates the importance of excise-tax effects.

Resource Allocation for Administration

THE OBJECT of property tax administration is to minimize some measure of inequality, I, of assessment-sales ratios subject to the constraint that total expenditures on administration, C, do not exceed the budget for administration, $\bar{C}$. The measure of inequality may take any of a wide variety of forms—the coefficient of dispersion or relative variance, for example, weighted by the value of the property, or unweighted. In general, I might well depend on the coefficient of variation $\sigma^* (= \sigma/\mu)$, of the distribution of rates of change of property values, where σ is the standard deviation and μ the mean of that distribution; the average assessment lag, L, which equals the number of assessments per period divided by the number of properties; and a measure of the accuracy of assessments, such as the coefficient of variation of the assessments around market value, a^*. Thus $I = f(\sigma^*, L, a^*)$.

The object of the assessing administration is to maximize $U = h(I) = h[f(\sigma^*, L, a^*)] = F(\sigma^*, L, a^*)$, subject to the constraint that $\bar{C} \geq C$, where the assessment lag and quality determine C; that is, $C = g(L, a^*)$, or

(B-1) $$\text{Max } Z = F(\sigma^*, L, a^*) + \lambda [\bar{C} - g(L, a^*)],$$

where λ is a Lagrangian multiplier.

The first-order conditions require that

$$\frac{F_L}{g_L} = \frac{F_{a^*}}{g_{a^*}};$$

and since

$$F_L = h_I f_L \text{ and } F_{a^*} = h_I f_{a^*},$$

they also require

(B-2) $$\frac{f_L}{g_L} = \frac{f_{a*}}{g_{a*}}.$$

In other words, the ratios of the marginal reductions in I due to lower L or lower a^* must be proportional to the marginal costs of achieving these changes. In general, assessors may care unequally about changes in I for different classes of property, and the costs of assessing different classes of property may differ, so that

$$U = h(I_1, \ldots, I_n) = F(\sigma_1^*, L_1, a_1^*, \ldots, \sigma_n^*, L_n, a_n^*)$$

and

$$C = \sum_{i=1}^{n} g^i(L_i, a_i^*),$$

where each property class, i, includes units whose incorrect assessments are valued equally and whose cost of appraisal is identical. The i may run over value classes, locations, property types, race or wealth of tenants, or any other characteristic. In that case the first-order conditions become

(B-2a) $$\frac{f_{L_i} h_{I_i}}{g_{L_i}} = \frac{f_{L_j} h_{I_j}}{g_{L_j}} = \frac{f_{a_i^*} h_{I_j}}{g_{a_i^*}} = \frac{f_{a_j^*} h_{I_j}}{g_{a_j^*}}   (i, j = 1, \ldots, n).$$

The operational job of administering any tax consists of the following tasks:

(a) Specify the function h, that is, the disutility from inaccurately assessing various categories of properties.

(b) Define I, since the particular indicator of inequality may affect the ordering of property types according to degree of inequality and may affect the optimal values of L_i and a_i^*.

Decisions (a) and (b) are both clearly political, since they will affect the quantity of resources devoted to administering the tax on various groups and the relative emphasis on accuracy versus frequency of assessment. Given the function h and a measure I, the function F is defined and yields the social utility of a decline in I.

(c) Find values of dI/dL and dI/da_i^*. The estimation of dI/dL, given a defined measure I and initial assessed values, depends on the change in market prices. These can be estimated by the same procedures used in the computer-based reassessments mentioned in the text. Let P_{it} be the change in price of property of type i from period $t - 1$ to period t. Then

(B-3) $$P_{it} = \sum_j a_{ij} D_{ij} + E_{it}   i = (1, \ldots, n),$$

where the D_{ij} are j characteristics of property of type i and E_{it} is a $(0, \sigma)$ error term. The D_{ij} can include data on value class, location, past price change, or any other characteristic deemed appropriate. If the relationships expressed in equation (B-3) are assumed to remain stable, (B-3) can be used for forecasting property values, using actual or projected values of the D_{ij}. At the same time it is possible to estimate a^* from past assessments followed promptly by sales. The difficulty here is estimating the cost of changing a^*.

A decision to reassess every $\bar{L}$ periods rather than every $(\bar{L} - 1)$ periods results in administrative savings of $(C_{\bar{L}-1} - C_{\bar{L}})$ dollars and increases inequality by $(I_{\bar{L}} - I_{\bar{L}-1})$. A decision to reassess every $\bar{L}$ periods rather than $(\bar{L} + 1)$ periods costs $(C_{\bar{L}} - C_{\bar{L}+1})$ dollars and decreases inequality by $(I_{\bar{L}+1} - I_{\bar{L}})$. The allocation of assessing resources between reducing the lag and increasing accuracy is optimal if $(I_{\bar{L}+1} - I_{\bar{L}})$ is greater than the reduction in I that would be obtained from applying $(C_{\bar{L}} - C_{\bar{L}+1})$ to reducing a^*, but $(I_{\bar{L}} - I_{\bar{L}-1})$ is less than the deduction in I that would be obtained from applying $(C_{\bar{L}-1} - C_{\bar{L}})$ to reducing a^*. If the distribution of resources between reducing L and a^* is optimal, letting V_L be $(C_{L-1} - C_L)/(I_L - I_{L-1})$ and V the value that tax administrators place on inequality, then

$$V_L > V > V_{L+1}.$$

It is quite simple to construct illustrative distributions of assessment-sales ratios yielding different values of I and to explain to those who set the budget for property tax administration the cost of achieving these distributions by varying L and a^*.

In fact, the advent of computer-based reassessments means that administrators must choose between on-site appraisals and statistical analysis. Furthermore, the appeals process also affects I and C and should be included in the calculation.

One would expect that I would vary across jurisdictions according to the variance of the growth of properties; furthermore, property mixes differ, and for each type of property in the mix, concern about the accuracy of assessments differs and so do the costs of assessment.

Index

Aaron, Henry J., 2n, 32n, 51n, 53n, 61n, 69n, 76n, 77n

Administration, property tax, 3, 4, 92; arguments for reform in, 64–65, 67; expenditures for, 63–64; factors working against reform in, 66–67; evaluated by coefficient of dispersion, 15–17; proposals for, 57, 69–70, 94, 95; role of tax assessor in, 61–62; tax concessions and, 62. *See also* Assessment

Advisory Commission on Intergovernmental Relations, 4, 14, 25, 64, 68n, 75n

Aged: circuit-breaker plan for, 74; property tax exemption for, 71, 72, 94; tax deferral for, 77, 94

Ando, Albert, 29n

Assessment, 3, 4; full disclosure of, 69, 94; intentional discrimination in, 59–62; procedures for, 7–8; proposed reforms in, 69–70; unintentional discrimination in, 63–64; at uniform percentage of market value, 14. *See also* Reassessment

Assessment-sales ratio, 63, 69

Austin, John S., 32n

Bailey, Martin J., 51n
Balk, Alfred, 81n, 84n
Bannink, R., 51n
Beck, Ralph A., 66n
Bendick, Marc, Jr., 74, 78
Bittker, Boris I., 82
Blinder, Alan S., 49n

Boston, property tax administration, 60–61

Brady, Ronald W., 65n
Break, George F., 49n
Brown, Harry Gunnison, 2n
Brumberg, Richard, 29n
Bureau of the Census, 34
Burnham, James B., 32n
Business property tax, 7, 45, 60, 87

California; educational financing, 4; system of computer-based reassessment, 69

Capital: changes in tax rates on, 51–52; effect of property tax on rate of return of, 43, 45, 49; industry variations in taxation of, 52–53; mobility of, 41, 42; tax shifting and, 20, 38–40

Capital gains or losses, in property values, 64

Capital improvements, 39–40

Capitalization, of property tax differentials, 57–59, 62, 64, 80

Capital stock, effect of property taxation on, 50

Carliner, Geoffrey, 32n

Charitable organizations, property tax exemption for, 7, 81

Church, Albert M., 66n

Circuit-breaker plans: explanation of, 72; grant system versus, 78–79; as income maintenance plan, 75–76, 78; objective of, 74–75; to reduce property tax regressiveness, 74; for renters, 77; tax deferral plan versus, 77–78

DATE DUE